The 45-Day
Investor

Can we file an
ammendment to
last years
(2014) taxes
by claiming my
daughters?

The 45-Day Investor

How to buy an investment property with nothing down in 45 days or less

Kevin Amolsch

ISBN: 0692501193
ISBN 13: 9780692501191

CONTENTS

INTRODUCTION

The year was 2002. I was 23 years old, and I already had one rental property. I knew that I would make my fortune in real estate, but at this rate, it would take me 60 years. I needed to buy houses faster. It was already almost a year since I'd turned my old house into a rental, and it took me two years to get that done. My now-ex-wife, Steph, and I were ready to try our first creative real estate deal and definitely had the guts to do it. What we were lacking was the knowledge. I found a seller who was motivated to sell but wanted $3,000 in cash to transfer the title. I brought in a partner, and we gave him his $3,000 and took title to the house. There was a mortgage in place that was more than the value, so we started to negotiate with the lender to accept less than what was owed. The problem, of course, was that they were not willing to negotiate. Countrywide Home Loans ended up with the house, and we ended up with a $3,000 lesson. From that point forward, I knew that if I was ever going to make a fortune (which is not that hard to do), I needed to understand how to structure deals. In this book I will share with you how to find, negotiate, and structure your deals so that you never learn the $3,000 lesson.

I first want to thank you for taking the time to read this book. You may be hoping that by reading this, you will get past a barrier in your investing. Maybe you are hoping to pick up a few tips or ideas. Or maybe you are just reading this because you know the only way to grow and succeed is to consistently feed your mind information. Whatever your objective, I am proud and humbled that you chose this book and promise to do my best to give you the value you are looking for.

The primary goal of this book is to explain how you can buy your first (or next) investment property in the next 45 days. You will learn the exact steps to take and what pitfalls to look out for. I will explain some of the biggest mistakes that I have made, which have cost me thousands and thousands of dollars. You will also learn about my first deals and a few successes. One of the most important things you can learn is that the easiest way to accomplish anything is to copy someone who has done it successfully. My hope is that by reading this, you will copy some of the things I have done and am currently doing so that you can experience similar success. I know the steps in this book work because these are the steps I used when I began investing in real estate. This book shares my story of how I became successful in real estate and how you can too.

After graduating high school, I went into the US Army for three years. I bought my first home in 2000, shortly after my 21st birthday and several months before I was discharged from the army. Life was great. My best friend from high school, Ryan, was already living in the house I bought when I decided to leave the army in pursuit of college, parties, and girls. Ryan and I were very close, and I could not wait to finally have a cool roommate after living with some of the army guys. I'm only kidding; I had great roommates in the army, but this was different—this was my best friend. We lived together for a few days before he left to move in with his future wife. Sometimes girls have a way of changing an old friend's plans. Just when you think you know a guy! Luckily, Ryan wasn't my only friend, and I had a new roommate in no time.

My new roommate, Anthony, and I lived in that house for almost two years while I went to school and worked at a bank as a customer service representative. Although I became friends with Ricky, the gang member next door, I decided to move out of the neighborhood. I decided this partly because it was in my long-term real estate strategy and partly because I had a new female friend in my life, and I needed to impress her.

I met Stephanie at the bank I worked at right before I moved from the "ghetto," as she would put it. Steph and I had a lot in common and made a connection right away. She has moved on to new adventures, but real estate is really what brought us together in the beginning. You will notice I say "us" or "we" a lot, because aside from my first two houses, she and I worked closely together in the beginning. Without her help and support, I would not have the businesses that I do today.

Today I run a large hard-money-lending company based in Colorado. I am a proud father to two beautiful girls who bring so much joy and happiness to my life. They are still young, but I cannot wait to get them going in real estate too.

That first home, which I recently sold, is in an area of Denver considered by many to be a war zone, and for good reason. There were several shootings nearby while I lived there. (See why Steph was not impressed?)

Before I moved into my second home, I decided that I was going to use real estate to become rich. Since then I have been directly involved with over 150 real estate transactions as a buyer or seller and another 900 as a private money lender. I have purchased homes using conventional methods, short sales, subject to the existing financing, and lease options. I have purchased properties from owners, banks, private lien holders, estates, and other real estate investment companies. I have flipped contracts, flipped seller referrals, flipped buyer referrals, and fixed and flipped houses. I wanted to try as many different ways to do things as I could so I could grow and learn the best and easiest ways to make money.

In the following sections, you will learn some basics about investing in real estate and some specific strategies you can use to build a cash-flowing rental portfolio as I did.

THE NUTS AND BOLTS

WHY REAL ESTATE?

You have undoubtedly heard that more millionaires created their wealth through real estate than any other investment vehicle. This is true! There is not one wealth guru I have studied who did not do some real estate investing. In fact, even friends and family or other people I meet on a day-to-day basis who have dabbled in real estate seem to be better off financially than those who have not. Think about the people in your life who have purchased at least one property for an investment compared to those who have not. Do you notice a difference in their financial lives? Choosing real estate to create wealth was an easy decision for me after watching late-night TV. I have always wondered what percentage of people buy something from late-night TV in a sober state of mind. Sunday morning at 3:00 a.m. seems to be a great time to run influential marketing shows, and I happened to be one of the suckers to buy a course at that time. I did not purchase a real estate course, but I did purchase a course on financial education that focused on creating passive income. The course got me excited about real estate and made me want to look into it further.

> *Real estate may be the most forgiving investment one can make. Because there is a limited supply of land, real estate will appreciate over time.*

In my opinion, you cannot lose in real estate as long as you are in it for the long haul. It is OK to make mistakes because real estate is an extremely forgiving investment. There is a finite amount of land, creating a limited amount of supply, and there will always be demand because people need houses. With supply being limited and a demand that increases over time, values must go up. At times we will see market adjustments where price appreciation will flatten or even decrease, like we did during the credit crunch, but these adjustments are only temporary, and the market always recovers.

Price appreciation alone does not make real estate a great investment. There are many other advantages to consider, including high leverage, tax benefits, equity, monthly cash flow, and safety. Plus, it's fun.

High Leverage

When I say high leverage, I am referring to using other people's money. The key to wealth is the ability to leverage other people's money and time. In real estate, you can literally have infinite returns on your investment because you can buy property using none of your own money. Even if you do use a down payment, it is not unusual to see cash-on-cash returns of over 100 percent a year.

Let's look at an example in its simplest form. I purchased my first house for $100,000. After I owned the home for one year, it was worth $110,000. That is an increase of 10 percent over the year. If I wrote a check for the purchase, I would have made a 10 percent return on my investment. This is calculated by taking the profit of $10,000 and dividing it by the investment of $100,000.

$$\$110{,}000 - \$100{,}000 = \$10{,}000 \text{ profit}$$
$$\$10{,}000 \: / \: \$100{,}000 = 10\% \text{ return}$$

What I actually did was use a Federal Housing Administration (FHA) loan, putting down 3 percent and taking out a loan for the other 97 percent. This made my return on investment 333 percent.

$$\$110,000 - \$100,000 = \$10,000 \text{ profit}$$
$$\$10,000 / \$3,000 = 333\% \text{ return}$$

If I knew then what I know now, I could have easily purchased this house with no money down, which would have made my return infinite.

I understand that with other investments like stocks or businesses, you can use leverage in the form of loans, margin accounts, and other strategies, but it is much easier to finance real estate.

Tax Benefits

Boredom alert! If, like most people, you hate the subject of taxes, you may want to skip this section. However, these benefits are huge and make a big difference in your taxable income, so I feel it is important to spend just a little time in this area.

The government needs landlords to help provide safe and affordable housing. For this reason, they pay us in the form of tax breaks for owning property. I have done my fair share of studying tax laws, and I work with an accountant to help me take all the deductions allowed. My suggestion would be to find a competent accountant with expertise in real estate to help, but you should strive to understand the deductions that your accountant helps you take each year.

This is a business and should be treated as such. All expenses related to your business should be deductible. This includes obvious ones like interest on your mortgage, your property taxes, your insurance premiums, and property maintenance. It also includes expenses to find the properties, like marketing materials, postage, and referral fees.

Some other deductions you may not realize are property depreciation, car mileage, expenses related to your home office, and meals and entertainment.

Property Depreciation

Depreciating property for tax deductions is a confusing subject for many investors. The IRS rules say that a property depreciates in value over time. The amount of time is considered the useful life, or life expectancy. The assumption is that if the owner of the property does not take care of it, the property will become worthless. At the time of writing this book, the useful life of a piece of residential property is 27.5 years. Because the IRS considers the property to be losing value, it allows us to deduct an equal portion of our tax basis each year. We cannot deduct the value of the land because the dirt does not lose value like the structure will. It is a bit more complicated than this, but a basic example would be if we purchased a home for $100,000, and the value of the land is considered to be $20,000, we would depreciate $80,000 over 27.5 years. Our tax deduction would be $2,909 per year.

$$\$80,000 \: / \: 27.5 \text{ years} = \$2,909 \text{ per year}$$

One thing we need to understand is that the IRS requires us to take this depreciation on rental property. We have no choice. Also, it is important to know that we will need to recapture the depreciation when we liquidate the home. This will increase our capital gains each year because our tax basis is reducing. A capital gain is the difference between what the property is sold for and the basis. Using our same example, let's say we sell the home for $120,000 three years later. Our basis started at $100,000 and reduced by $2,909 for three years. Our capital gain will be $28,727.

$2,909 x 3 years = $8,727 (depreciation)
$100,000 (beginning basis) –$8,727 (depreciation) = $91,273 (new basis)
$120,000 (sell price) - $91,273 (new basis) = $28,727 (capital gain)

This is where it can get really confusing. If you don't need the tax write-off, you will want to depreciate the property as slowly as possible, so you will depreciate everything other than land over 27.5 years.

However, if you need deductions because you have a lot of income, you can depreciate different parts of the property at different rates. For example, from the land value, you will want to break out bushes,

Did you know with a good CPA you have some control over the amount of depreciation you can take each year?

fences, and landscaping and depreciate those to reduce the land value as much as possible. You will also want to break out different parts of the property, like the carpet, appliances, and fixtures, which have shorter life expectancies and can be depreciated much faster.

Here is a list of what can be broken out of the property in order to depreciate items faster and increase your tax benefits.

Most personal property (carpet, window coverings, appliances, etc...)	5 years
Furniture and Fixtures	7 years
Land improvements (fences, landscaping, sidewalks, etc...)	15 years
Sewers	20 years
Everything else including the structure	27.5 years

I also want to point out that although you do have to recapture the depreciation amount, you are likely shifting ordinary income to capital gain. For most investors, this is moving income from a higher tax percentage to a lower one. Depending on how you do your taxes, the depreciation is used to offset income, possibly even income that is earned outside of real estate. If you are in a high tax bracket, this could benefit you greatly. When you recapture it, it may be considered capital gain and will be taxed at a much lower rate.

Please don't get hung up on this, but now you can see why it is important to include a competent CPA on your team as soon as you buy your first investment property.

Car Mileage

There are two ways to take a tax benefit from car mileage. One is to deduct all the expenses related to the business, and the other is to take a deduction per business mile driven. In either case, you will need good records of the number of miles you drove for personal reasons and the amount you drove for business. I don't want to get into too much detail here, but generally you will get a larger deduction if you deduct the expenses. However, this creates a lot more records because you will need receipts for all car-related expenses, including gas and maintenance.

A good CPA will help you decide which way makes more sense in your situation. I personally need tax deductions, so my company owns my car and pays for all the gas and maintenance, but I need to keep track of personal miles used because that amount is not deductible.

Expenses Related to a Home Office

This is a touchy subject, and from my understanding, an area closely scrutinized by the IRS. For this reason, many investors will not bother taking these deductions because to them it is not worth the risk of an audit. Other investors will push the limit and keep good records in case there is an audit.

The way this works is that all expenses related to running a home office for your business are deductible. This includes utilities, insurance premiums, taxes, and maintenance. The expenses are broken up depending on what percentage of the home is for business use and what percentage is for personal use. Let's say you use a bedroom for an office. This may be 15 percent of the home, so you will deduct 15 percent of related expenses as a business expense.

The catch here is that according to the IRS rule, you cannot use this part of your home for any other purpose. So you can't throw a computer in the corner of your bedroom and call it an office.

Meals and Entertainment

This is one of the IRS's favorite traps during an audit. You will want to take full advantage of these deductions, trust me, but you do not want to be caught without documentation of the events. I keep all receipts in a folder, and when I enter the expense into my books, I record who I was with and the purpose of the meeting. I have heard of other people just jotting this down on the back of the receipt. I may not be the best example, because I throw all my receipts in one folder. You may want to be more organized and have a different folder for each month or something similar to make it easier if you need to find a receipt.

Meals and entertainment are deductible to the extent that they are for a business purpose. For example, if you go look at properties in another state and then stay a few extra days to visit your mom, those few extra days are not deductible. It is also a red flag if you are taking the same people to happy hour every Friday. The expenses must be strictly related to the tax payer and the people involved in the business, meaning no pizza parties for your son's birthday.

These deductions are generally 50 percent deductible and have to meet three criteria:

1. There is more than a general hope of creating income or other business benefit from the meeting.
2. A bona fide business activity takes place.
3. The principal reason for the meal or entertainment is to conduct business.

Meals and entertainment are only considered 100 percent deductible when they fall under these categories: (a) wages or bonuses; (b) the convenience of the employer (like lunch when you make your employees work through lunch); and (c) entertainment for employees, such as a company picnic.

Because creating relationships is essential in this business, you will be taking people out to lunch. In fact, I would recommend you take someone to lunch no less than once a week. Keep good records, and deduct everything you can.

Equity

What I am talking about here is the difference between what you can sell the property for and what you owe. Unlike a stock, which sells for the value, you can buy real estate at a discount. This is instant equity because as soon as you buy the property, you have equity, and your personal net worth increases. We will get into the details of finding properties you can purchase for a discount later in the book.

There are three ways to increase your equity position in a property over time: appreciation, loan pay-down, and forced appreciation.

Appreciation

We will not spend much time on this subject because I have already touched on it. Real estate is a proven appreciating asset. It has always increased in value over time. As I mentioned, we could see values decrease for a short run, but they always recover. You can also increase your chances that a property you buy will appreciate at a faster rate by simply buying in the right areas. You have heard the saying "location, location, location." Residential real estate is extremely sensitive to location. I am referring to both areas of the country and areas of a city. Certain areas of the country will be doing well while others are not, but if you look within cities, you will see certain neighborhoods doing better than others. I have houses in a Denver neighborhood that have decreased in value by over 30 percent in a three-year span while some of my other properties in a Denver suburb have increased in value during the same time.

Getting to know areas takes a little time and a little work. Yes, you can research areas using tools like the US Census Bureau and try to time the market by looking at graphs, but you would be better off getting out and looking at homes and talking to people in the industry. You will find that everyone likes to talk about the market and what it's doing, and everyone seems to have a crystal ball, so you should have no problem getting people's opinions. You can find people to talk to by going to meetings attended by other investors, or you can simply pretend you are a tenant and call some "for rent" ads. Later we will discuss more extensively all the different ways to talk to others. Once you start buying and renting houses, you will get a feel for what prices and rents are doing.

One idea that may help increase your chances of rapid appreciation is to buy in areas where the city has construction planned. You can research city development plans on the city's website. People have become rich buying rentals along planned public transportation routes; however, it could take years for the city projects to be completed, so be prepared to hold these properties long-term.

With all this said, I do want to point out that you probably should not buy a piece of property based on your expectation of appreciation. I like to focus on cash flow and have the appreciation as a nice bonus. If a property's cash flow is positive, you can hold the property forever, so the market fluctuation is not as important. You will have total flexibility if and when you decide to sell.

Loan Pay-Down

This may sound like the most ridiculous thing ever, but there seems to be some controversy about this subject. With the loans and the strategies that are available to us, it can be confusing. Should you focus on paying down the loan fast, or should you try to drag it out?

There are advantages and disadvantages to both. In either case, my guess is that there will be a fully amortizing loan in place, so let's start by talking about the amortization schedule.

An amortization schedule is really a genius way to have a set monthly payment that will pay off the principal over a set period of time. Without the amortization schedule, your loan payment would change each and every month. People will tell you that the amortization schedule is a bad thing and is all weighted in the bank's favor. Although this is true, it is the *only* way to have a fixed monthly payment while reducing principal. You pay more of each payment in interest in the beginning because you owe more on the loan in the beginning. The interest portion of your fixed monthly payment is calculated based on the size of the loan, which should change each month as you pay it down.

I include a few graphs of amortization loans below. By looking at the amortization schedule, you can see how slowly you are reducing the principal in the beginning years. This is important to understand because you can benefit from this, which we will discuss later. For now I just want you to understand that you are paying down the mortgage with each payment as long as the loan is amortized, and it is rather slow in the beginning years.

The charts below are for a 30-year term, a loan amount of $200,000, and an interest rate of 6.5 percent. The monthly payment is $1,264. The first graph shows the life of the loan, which is 360 months, and the second graph indicates the first five years of the loan. I used five years to make my point because most people do not keep a loan longer than that. After five years, we have paid this loan down by $12,530 and still owe $187,470.

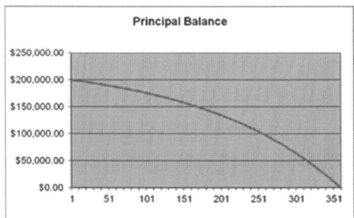

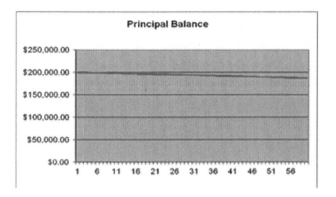

The longer you keep the property, the more you can take advantage of the amortization schedule. While you own and rent the home, the tenant will be paying off the loan for you.

Advantages

Some investors like to use strategies to pay off the loan at an accelerated pace. The advantage to this is that the cash flow will increase with no loan payment, and you will have a nice warm fuzzy that the property is free and clear. As we get older and want a more simple life, that warm fuzzy becomes much more valuable. If you choose to accelerate the loan payoff, there are a few ways to go about this. Obviously, paying extra each month or picking a shorter amortization schedule, like 10 or 15 years instead of 30, will work. There are, however, more creative and effective ways to do this as well. I am not the expert in this because I don't think paying off the mortgage is the best strategy for most investors, but if this is your goal, you need to check out the information from my friends at VIP Financial Education: www.DebtFreeClass.net.

Disadvantages

There are several disadvantages to paying off mortgages:

Restrictive. If you are in a financial growth phase of your life, which I assume you are since you are reading this, paying off your mortgages is restrictive.

Leverage is a key component to making real estate attractive, as I have mentioned. As you pay off your loans, your overall returns decrease. If you want your equity to work, you would pull the money out and invest it. The basic concept here is that if you can get a higher return on the money you borrow, you will benefit from the spread. Let's say you borrow the money on a rental property mortgage at 6 percent. You should easily be able to get returns of 25 percent or more leveraging into real estate. Let's use a house worth $100,000 as an example, and let's say you will buy this house as a rental with traditional financing, so you will have a $20,000 down payment. Let's further assume that you need $10,000 in additional capital to make some repairs before you can rent it and to cover closing costs. So you are into this house for $30,000 ($20,000 down payment plus $10,000 in repairs).

If you can borrow the other $80,000 at 6 percent, your monthly payment would be about $480 plus taxes and insurance. Let's assume your total monthly payment with taxes and insurance is $600 per month. That house in my market will rent for $850, maybe a little more, depending on the neighborhood. That creates a cash flow before maintenance and vacancy of $250 per month, or $3,000 a year. Now, let's assume that this property only appreciates at 5 percent a year. Over time, you should expect 5 percent to 7 percent appreciation, but there will be some fluctuation, so you need to have a long horizon to count on any appreciation. At 5 percent, that is a value increase of $5,000 in the first year. You also would have paid close to $1,000 of principal off your loan, creating more equity, assuming it was a 30-year loan. Here is how that investment would shake out in just the first year.

Cash Flow	$3,000.00
Appreciation	$5,000.00
Loan pay-down	$1,000.00
Total return	$9,000
Divide total return by your investment of $30,000: ($9,000 / $30,000)	30% annual return

15

This 30 percent return does not include the value increase from the $10,000 of improvements you made or the tax benefits you get from owning another piece of real estate. You should have instant equity of another $10,000 to $20,000, assuming you found a decent deal. I know this does not account for vacancy or maintenance that you will have, but it would be unlikely that you'll have much of that your first year. Even if your return is half of what you are expecting, it is still significantly higher than the amount you are paying to borrow the money. Using real estate equity to invest should speed up your financial growth significantly. Remember, equity in a home produces a 0 percent return. Many of my clients and friends actually refinance their properties every four or five years to pull the equity out and move it into other investments.

Exposure. Having equity in a home can create problems. From an asset-protection standpoint, equity in a home is at risk during a lawsuit. The sad reality in this business is that it is not a matter of "if"; it is a matter of "when" you get sued. Investors are viewed as having deep pockets, making them attractive for attorneys to go after. Many attorneys work on a contingency basis, meaning they don't get paid if they don't collect money. For this reason, they will only sue you if you have assets. If the properties you own have no equity, you are reducing your chance of getting sued.

Taxes. The last disadvantage is that you will be paying off a tax shelter. We have already talked about some of the tax benefits of having real estate debt. The interest is deductible. If you are not paying interest, you do not have the tax deduction. This is especially true under current tax law with your primary home. If you do choose to pay off debt, start with rentals. Your primary home generally has the lowest interest rate and the best tax benefit.

Forced Appreciation

We can literally force appreciation. This is one of the biggest reasons people get into the real estate investing business. The two primary ways to force appreciation are: (a) to make repairs or improvements and (b) to sell the home on terms. This appreciation is in addition to any discount you are able to negotiate when you buy the property.

A lot of investors will buy a home that needs work for a good price just to fix it up and sell it. Taking the risk and rehabilitating a home forces the home to be worth more than the purchase price when you bought it. The key is to make the appropriate repairs. Many inexperienced investors will overspend or over-improve a house and not get the money back that they put in. The most successful flippers that I know understand what work adds the most value. There is a lot to this strategy that is outside the scope of this book. Our blog (www.PineFinancialGroup.com/blog) is loaded with information for people interested in fixing and flipping houses. If you are doing fixes and flips in an area in which we loan, be sure to consider our 100 percent rehab loan to buy and fix a house with no down payment.

I love the idea of buying a home that needs work and fixing it up enough to rent it. This is the best way to buy a home that will generate cash flow and give you instant equity. It is much easier than flipping the house, because you don't need to do as much to get the property ready to rent.

Another great way to force appreciation is to sell the home on terms. You don't need much skill as an investor to make money doing this. I have talked to several investors who really do not know much about real estate yet still make money. You can pay full price for a home, do no repairs, and sell it as a rent to own or owner financing for more than you paid for it simply because you are offering attractive financing. I have seen people make $10,000, $20,000, or more per deal, paying full price for a home and using this strategy. We will dig into this concept in detail later, but it is good to understand now that the type of financing or terms of the sale are just as important as price when buying and selling homes.

Monthly Cash Flow

This could be the most obvious reason many investors buy rental property. There are several things to look for when you are searching for an investment. In my opinion, cash flow is the number one most critical component. Like I mentioned earlier, as long as you have cash flow, you can stay in the game and wait out any market swings or mistakes you may have made. With zero or negative cash flow, your investment could be a ticking time bomb of bankruptcy disaster.

Cash flow is the difference between the cash you receive and the cash you pay out. I would refer to any investment you make that does not have positive cash flow as being speculative. Speculating is very risky but could pay off handsomely. If you can afford it, there is nothing wrong with speculating. In fact, many expert investors will tell you to keep some speculative investments in your portfolio. I do not recommend doing that when you are first getting started. Save the guesswork until you have money you can afford to lose.

One of the greatest things about rents on property is that they increase over time, so as you hold property, you will be able to increase your total monthly cash flow without working. Wouldn't it be great to give yourself a raise every year and not work harder for it? I love the first part of the month when I see my bank accounts grow. Rental property is not entirely passive, but you don't need to work that hard to make a ton of money.

Safety

Real estate is one of the safest investments you can make. You will hear people say real estate is risky and that you have to really know what you are doing to play the game. That is the biggest load of garbage I have ever heard. I am also an active investor in the stock market, and I can tell you I have stocks that are moving up and down every day. I bought a stock that was supposed to be a bargain buy. All the "experts" were saying it would increase in value over the next year. About two weeks after I bought the stock, a lawsuit was created by some copyright infringement, and the stock plummeted. I probably lost over 20 percent of my investment in less than an hour. Now that's risky!

I did lose 30 percent of the value of three properties I owned in a specific Denver neighborhood during the financial downturn. This indicates there are some obvious risks...or are there? I acquired all three of these houses with nothing down, and I have not sold any of them, so I have not lost anything. I am losing a little monthly on one of them, but the other two have positive cash flow that covers the difference. I do not have to sell any of them and will keep them until the value comes back. Chances are I will not lose a penny. Again, I made a mistake by buying in the wrong area, but I won't lose, because I have time to ride out the storm.

Investing in a bank account or money market fund may seem like the safest way to go. To some people it is, but to me that is the riskiest thing you can do. If you keep money in a bank, you are cutting off the oxygen to your financial future. Sure, you probably won't lose any of your investment, but you will be eroding money through inflation. Over time you are probably earning 1 percent or less in this type of investment. The average inflation rate over the last 50 years is 4.08 percent. Many believe we could see much higher inflation in the years to come. This would mean you are earning an effective −3.08 percent on your investment in the bank or a money market fund. You are actually losing buying power as you save money. That's disgusting!

If you are retired, need the money within a short period of time, or are not looking for a profit, by all means throw your money into the bank. Do not, however, commit financial suicide by saving for retirement or college or any other long-term goal this way.

Fun

Aside from the massive financial benefits of real estate, I decided to get into the business because it is fun. You can talk about real estate with other investors for days and not completely cover the subject. There is just too much you can do with it, and there are too many opportunities. Most people start with single-family homes. There are an infinite number of strategies you can use to buy someone's home, and there are an infinite number of ways you can sell it and make a profit. Your options are limited only by your creativity. In this business, every day you will experience and see something different. I can fill a book with the crazy things we have seen and the crazier people we have met. As you get calls from people trying to sell their homes, you start to realize that the business is so much more than buying property and making a lot of money. You are really performing a much-needed service to society. These people need our help, and it is a lot of fun coming up with solutions to solve their problems. In many cases, it comes down to a financial problem; you can look at yourself as a financial doctor or a financial problem solver.

For example, a house I recently sold was purchased through probate. We bought it from the son of a lady who had died. He was the only sibling in town, and he wanted to sell it to move closer to his sister and brother-in-law. He called us from a flyer we'd had the Boy Scouts put on his door about buying his home. He was trying to sell but was not having any luck because the house needed updating. He invited us over to have a look. After a brief phone conversation, I knew he was motivated, so I agreed to meet with him.

When we got to his home, he seemed to be in a good mood, but it was obvious he was hurting emotionally. We walked around his home and got to know him a little better while we got a chance to look around. Some minor work needed to be done but nothing major. The reason it was not selling was because, although the kitchen was updated, the counters and cabinets did not fit correctly. To be honest, I almost laughed when I walked into the kitchen. We sat down, and he told me he'd lost his dad a few years earlier, and his mom had just died. Suddenly, the funky kitchen was no longer funny. His mom was the only reason he was in Colorado, and he really wanted to get out of town. The problem was that he was responsible for liquidating his mother's house, and he did not want to even try after the problems he was having with his own house. He was done and wanted to move.

We followed him to his mom's place and looked through the home with him. It was the typical outdated home built about 35 years prior. The carpet was blue in some rooms and red in others. All the fixtures were dated, and there was a disgusting tile counter in the kitchen. There were additions everywhere. There were about 15 homemade sheds in the back. In fact, the entire backyard was sheds made of scraps from construction sites. The attached garage was becoming a detached garage—it was pretty much separated from the house. There was a bay window made of scrap glass doors in the front of the house. There was a 900-square-foot addition that was added illegally and was moving in its own direction (which was not the same direction as the rest of the house). Watermarks covered the ceiling. Can you picture this house? I had not planned on writing this book then, or I would have saved some pictures to share.

We sat at the antique kitchen table with the orange chandelier providing the light. I went through my typical process and drew out all his motivation for selling. After about 45 minutes, I asked him what he was hoping I could do for him.

He cried out, "Buy these shitty houses so I can move!" That was music to my ears.

"OK," I responded, "what are you hoping to get for them, and in the condition they are in, what do you realistically think they are worth?"

We negotiated on price for the next 15 minutes or so, and I ended up buying them both for steep discounts. He was thrilled. We closed in less than two weeks. He brought his sister and brother-in-law to the closing to meet me and then left town. They literally drove the moving truck to the closing. Steph and I saw the truck parked in the lot when we pulled in, and I remember telling her that it had to be his truck. He was so happy at that closing table and was telling silly jokes. We all laughed as we sat there eating cookies. We had a fantastic time.

I really felt great about the entire thing. I recently sold both of these, but they were in our portfolio for years. We purchased them with hard-money loans. The hard-money lender provided us the money to buy them and fix them up. Aside from the payments, we did not have a dime of our own money in either of these deals.

There are not many businesses that I know of where you can make a ton of money without much work and still help people.

You will also meet a lot of great people who work in the business. I met some of my best friends this way. Unlike so many other businesses, real estate really is a cooperative business. There are so many deals out there; investors can work together instead of competing. You need to get involved to know what I am talking about, but there really isn't much competition, and everyone has similar thought patterns, making it easier to get along and become friends. The best people with the biggest hearts are in this business. I love real estate.

LEASE-OPTION BASICS

I learned the basics of lease-option investing early on. When I was trying to figure out this whole real estate game, I went to a free evening seminar and received a copy of a book by Peter Conti and David Finkel entitled *How to Create Multiple Streams of Income: Buying Homes in Nice Areas with Nothing Down!* (Conti and Finkel 1999)

Lease Options are a great way to buy property without using any of your own money.

I came home that night excited to show off my new book. I don't think she really cared at the time, but Steph acted happy for me. That book ended up changing my life.

A lease option is a typical lease with the right to buy the home within a specified period of time. Unlike a sales contract or a purchase-and-sell agreement where both parties must perform, an option is a unilateral agreement. The person with the option has the right, *not* the obligation, to buy, but the grantor or optionor *must* sell. You can use a lease option to buy, you can use it to sell, or you can use it to buy and sell. If you use it to buy and sell, it is referred to as a "sandwich" lease option because you are sandwiched between two agreements.

Let's go through a few examples so you know exactly how this works and how you will profit.

Lease-Option Examples

Let's assume you were able to find a property owner moving out of state on a job transfer. We will call her Sally Seller. Sally has been trying to sell her home but has not had success because she did not have enough equity to use a Realtor. Now she is down to two weeks before she must move. You and Sally sit down and work out a deal where you are willing to lease the property from her for five years. You will guarantee payments and take care of most of the maintenance. You promise to pay her $1,000 per month. In return for your promises, she promises to sell you the home within the five years for $125,000. We can assume it is worth between $125,000 and $135,000 at the time you sign the agreement. Sally may not be able to continue making payments once she moves, so she really needs your help and understands you are an investor. She is allowing you to sublet and to resell *without* her permission and knows you will be making a profit.

You then find a new tenant who really wants to own a home but needs a little time to pay off some debt and improve his credit. We will call him Randy Resident. You decide to let Randy move into the home and will give him two years to buy at a price you lock in today. Because you are locking in a price and cannot sell to anyone else, you ask him to give you $5,000 in nonrefundable option consideration. He agrees to pay you $1,200 per month. Here is how the deal would look.

	Agreement with Sally	Agreement with Randy	Profit
Option Payment	$ -	$5,000	$5,000
Monthly Payment	$1,000	$1,200	$4,800
Purchase Price	$125,000	$140,000	$10,000
Term	60 months	24 months	
Total			$19,800.00

The $5,000 Randy gave you up front is credited toward the purchase, so you cannot count it as profit between your price with Sally and your price with Randy. This is why in the chart above you see a $10,000 profit instead of $15,000. You can lock in a price slightly higher than the current value because you are locking in a price for two years and offering it with terms. Your monthly cash flow will be $200 per month for 24 months. All maintenance you agree to with Sally will pass to Randy, so you should have little to no maintenance responsibility. As you can see, you put no money down and will make a profit of $19,800 over two years.

What if you want to give the tenant a portion of his or her rent as credit toward buying the home? This is a great tool to increase cash flow. Going through the same example, you and Randy agree that if he pays $100 extra per month, you will give him $200 every month toward the purchase.

	Agreement with Sally	Agreement with Randy	Profit
Option Payment	$ -	$5,000	$5,000
Monthly Payment	$1,000	$1,300	$7,200
Rent Credit	$ -	$200	($4,800)
Purchase Price	$125,000	$140,000	$5,200
Term	60 months	24 months	
Total			$12,600

As you can see, your monthly cash flow increases, but your total profit will decrease. This is OK because monthly cash flow is very, very important, especially if you are just getting started.

I get these questions all the time:

"What are the chances Randy will actually buy?"

"What if Randy does not buy?"

Less than 15 percent of my tenants buy the property. I used to invest a great deal of time trying to help my tenants qualify. I would give them information about how to improve their credit and call and check in from time to time. I would also keep copies of cancelled checks in their file to provide to lenders. With all that effort, most of my tenants still did not buy. Now I explain the risk of losing their option money and what it will take to qualify before they move in. From there it is sink or swim. There is only so much I can do, and we are all adults making our own decisions, so it is up to them to perform.

The good news is you will usually make more money if they don't buy. From the same example above, we will assume your first tenant does not buy at the end of the two years, but your second tenant does. Remember you have five years before you need to decide to buy or not, so you will have about three years remaining after Randy moves out. Our new tenant buyer is named Rachelle Resident.

	Agreement with Sally	Agreement with Rachelle	Profit
Option Payment	$ -	$5,000	$5,000
Monthly Payment	$1,000	$1,450	$10,800
Rent Credit	$ -	$200.00	($4,800)
Purchase Price	$125,000	$155,000.00	$25,000
Term	36 months	24 months	
Forfeited Option Consideration			$5,000
Previous Monthly Cash Flow			$7,200
Total			$48,200

We can immediately see our profit goes way up on the deal. In average market conditions, we will have the ability to increase the rent over time, and the value of the home will have increased. Rachelle agrees to pay you $1,450 per month for $200 rent credit, and the price of the home increased to $155,000. Remember Randy gave you $5,000 when he moved in, which was nonrefundable, so we add that to your total profit. You also received a monthly cash flow from Randy, so we need to add that to your total profits. Finally, we reduced the term of the agreement with Sally to 36 months, since that is what will be remaining. Nothing else with Sally changes.

If Rachelle does not buy, you will need to make a decision to buy the property from Sally Seller or to not buy, in which case Sally will regain control of the property. Or you can try to renegotiate a better deal. If the home did increase in value over the five years, chances are you will either buy it or quickly sell the property to someone at a discount. For example, if Rachelle moved out, and the home went up in value another $15,000 during her two-year agreement, the property would be worth about $170,000. You would still have the option to buy the home at $125,000. This would leave you with $45,000 in equity to work with.

As you can see, this works well in a market where property values are increasing. You still make money in a decreasing market, but it is more difficult, and you will actually make more if your first tenant buys. Also, the longer term you can get with the seller, the more times you can resell it to tenant buyers and the more money you can make. A long term with the seller is also important to further reduce your risk. The risk you are really trying to protect is opportunity costs because there is no market risk in this type of deal. I will normally sign 10-year deals with my sellers, giving me plenty of time to deal with the property and make some money.

When the market started to crash in 2007 and 2008, Stephanie and I had over 30 active lease options with sellers. As the values declined and our options started to expire, I called the sellers and started the negotiations over. More than half the time, the seller wanted to extend our deal with new terms. Typically, we got a lower monthly payment with more time and occasionally even got a better price. If we did not get a deal that we wanted, we would simply return the house to the seller and move on.

This year I will be giving another property back to the seller. I've had this house for 10 years, and the value now is $265,000, or maybe a little more, and our option price is $245,000. That is not enough room for me to do anything with, and the owner feels like she can sell it and get the $245,000 that we were going to pay. She is probably right, so it is a better situation for both of us to unravel our agreement. I had a net cash flow on this house of over $700 a month for several years, so it was a good deal for me, and we were able to get her out of the mortgage payment that she desperately needed out of 10 years ago. I also sold that house on a rent to own four different times, collecting $5,000 to $7,000 each time for additional profit. Obviously, it would have been better if the market had actually improved over the 10 years, but it is nice to know you can get out of the deal with no risk if you won't make any money.

In another example, I just renegotiated a deal with Jason. I have been making Jason's mortgage payment of about $1,000 a month for the last 10 years. The term expired, and Jason wanted his money. I have had the same tenant in place for all 10 years, paying us a little more than $1,200 a month. I have never received a maintenance request from the tenant. Further, the value of the home has increased, but the tenant is still not ready to buy. He recently started his own business, which disqualifies him for a conventional loan. I mentioned to Jason that the tenant is asking for a few more years. Reluctantly, he agreed. This gives me the time to get the tenant qualified. When he buys, I should net somewhere around $50,000.

Cashing Out

There are several ways to close this transaction with Randy or Rachelle and cash you out of the deal. You cannot sell a home you don't own, so here are a few ways to do this.

If you are not worried about disclosing your profit to both Sally and either Randy or Rachelle, it is best to let Sally close directly with them. You will coordinate a contract between Sally and Rachelle for the price you agreed to sell the home for. Working with a title company, you will disclose your profit within the closing documents that everyone signs and will be paid directly from the title company. Your profit is disclosed on what is called the settlement statement in the form of a payoff. If this was done right, you will have a lien on title that will need to be removed, and you will be asked to provide a payoff number to the title company. They will collect that money and pay you when you release the lien. If you use this strategy, you may consider having a licensed agent do the contract for you.

The second way to do this is to buy the house and resell it. If you are sure that Rachelle is going to buy, you can buy the property several months before Rachelle buys from you. Only do this if you won't mind owning the property in case Rachelle does not buy.

A third way to do it is to buy the home the same day Rachelle buys from you. This is referred to as a "simultaneous close" or a "double close." You will literally buy the home and sell the home at the same time. You are actually on title for less than a minute. You will be in a separate room with Sally at the title company and sign all the documents putting you on title. You will then go to another room with Rachelle and sign all the documents putting her on title. The title company records the deed in your name and then immediately records the deed in Rachelle's name. The great thing about this is you may not need a loan. Rachelle's loan could fund the entire transaction.

The simultaneous close is a little confusing and, honestly, is getting a *lot* harder to do. Lenders do not like these because the loan must go through underwriting before the seller (you in this example) is even on title. You must work with a good title company and with a lender willing to do this. I recommend either buying the home a month or two before you sell it (you will need to get a loan), or let Sally sell the home directly to Rachelle, and you disclose your profit on the settlement statement.

A fourth way to do this is to set up an entity that would be used just for this one deal. The entity could be an LLC, but I would recommend a trust. The original seller will be the owner of the entity but can transfer it to you the day of closing with your buyer. That way the owner of record, which is the trust or the LLC, is selling the house. The great thing about doing it this way is that it will work every time, and you do not need to disclose profit. The cons are the following:

- It is a little harder to explain to the seller but possible.
- There could be more fees to set this up. I would recommend using an attorney to do this.
- You will need to establish a bank account for the entity to cash your checks.

If you decide this is a strategy you want to use to make some extra money, I would recommend you keep your system as simple as possible at first. Once you know this is going to work for you, go ahead and spend the money to put a more complex but more appropriate system in place as described above.

Some final thoughts on cashing out your seller if your tenant does not buy. Assuming there is equity, some things you could consider include the following:

- List it with a Realtor.
- Sell it yourself, or buy it yourself and keep it long-term.
- Even easier, choose to assign your option to another investor for a fee.

RENT TO OWN

Before we get into the nitty-gritty about how to acquire property, I want to touch on dealing with tenants. It is essential that you know what you are going to do with a property *before* you buy it.

Why Rent to Own?

Like we talked about in the appreciation section, by making a home easier to own, you add value. When you hear the commercials about "buy now, pay later" or "easy financing," be assured you are paying more for that product than you would if you paid cash. There is no difference with real estate.

The reason this works is that you automatically increase the pool of buyers by offering to people who

Whenever you can increase the number of buyers you will increase the value of the home. By offering a home with terms you are forcing instant appreciation.

can qualify and people who can't quite qualify. A larger pool of buyers to choose from makes it easier to sell at the price you want.

The increased price is somewhat irrelevant because very few tenants with an option to buy a home actually exercise their option. As I mentioned before, most of the time they will simply walk away from their down payment and give you back the house. That being said, you should always price your properties high enough to make a decent profit if they do buy, while being fair to them.

The primary reasons I love rent to own include option consideration, better tenants, higher rents, little or no maintenance expense or hassle, and transferring of utilities.

Option Consideration

You will also hear this called "option payment" and "down payments." I hesitate calling it "down payments" because that's not really what it is. A down payment means they are buying the home. An option payment means they have the option to buy the home, and they need to pay something up front for the right to do so. Of course the option payment works like a down payment if they buy the home, because you will credit it toward the purchase, but it is nonrefundable if they don't buy. If I buy a stock option and the stock price goes down, I let my option expire and lose the money I paid for the right to buy the stock. There is no difference here. A premium can be charged to give someone the right to buy the property.

I like option payments because they make the tenants have something at risk, and they will typically care more about the property and the situation. Also, if they decide to move out, you can keep the money to help cover damages and to make a profit.

[handwritten note: applied to the price if you exercise your op. & buy]

Better Tenants

When I am renting a home, the rent-to-own tenants are usually great tenants. I have very few who don't pay and even fewer who don't take care of the home. Yes, there are always bad apples that slip through your screening, and you need to prepare for that, but for the most part, these are great tenants.

The option money helps here because they do not want to lose their money. If they default on the lease, the option will void, and they don't want that either. It is not usually necessary, but you can always remind the tenants what is at risk.

Higher Rents

Generally, tenants are willing to pay a little higher rent because they know they have a chance to own the home. It is easier to bump rents up by offering rent credits. A rent credit is a portion of the rent that is applied to buying the home. It's like paying a small portion of principal on the mortgage. I will generally match the additional rent they pay. For example, I may start my rent price at $1,295. If tenants choose, they can pay this amount, but they will not get any rent credit. If they want to pay $100 more per month, I will credit them $200 toward the purchase. If they pay $200 more a month, I will credit $400. So if they choose to pay $1,495 a month, each one-time payment will get them $400 off the purchase price. In this example, I just increased my cash flow by $200 per month. You can be more or less aggressive with your rent credits. When I have had the equity, I have offered 50 percent rent credits. So if they pay $1,600, I will give them $800 toward buying the home. I know there are some investors that will do 100 percent credit.

I also increase cash flow by loaning them some of their option payment. I always get at least half down. I recently signed up tenants on a rent to own, and I wanted $5,000 down. They gave me a cashier's check for $2,500 plus

Interesting strategy if little option consists available

the monthly payment and signed a note for the other $2,500. I am nice enough to give them an interest-free loan for 12 months. You, of course, can charge interest if you want. I would have been happy with the $2,500 down and having my vacancy taken care of, but I was able to increase my cash flow on this property by over $200 per month for the next year. They are very happy because I wanted the $5,000 down—at least that is how I advertised it—and they got in for $2,500. That is a win-win deal.

The tenants' intention is to buy the home. They care for it as if it were theirs. They also have more to lose because they put money down and have been building equity as they rented.

Little or No Maintenance Expense or Hassle

Another reason I love using a rent to own is that I pass the maintenance on to the tenants. Hey, they are buying the home, so they need to take care of it when something breaks. I do, however, step in if something major, like a furnace, breaks. This makes being a landlord easy, and I have never once had a tenant question this when he or she signed the lease. If you are like me and want to know when there is a major problem, you can always either buy a home-warranty policy or negotiate with the sellers that if something major goes wrong, they will need to help. I have asked sellers to step in and help on occasion. The bottom line is if you buy a home on a lease option and sell on a rent to own (rent to own and lease option are the same thing), you can structure it so you never pay for a repair.

Transfer Utilities

The last reason I love rent to own is you transfer all utilities to the tenant's name. Oftentimes it is expected that the owner will pay the water and trash bill for a rental but not on a rent to own. The new buyer is expected to pay all utilities. You can also transfer other fees like HOA (homeowners' association) dues.

THE 45-DAY INVESTOR

HOW TO BUY YOUR FIRST (OR NEXT) REAL ESTATE INVESTMENT IN 45 DAYS OR LESS!

O K, let's get down and dirty. So far we have talked basics. In this next section, you will learn step-by-step how to buy a piece of investment real estate.

Focus on a Strategy

You will want to have a pinpoint focus when you are getting started. Sure, there are multiple ways to buy property, and yes, it is good to know them, but you must first master one area before you move to the next. This is not a get-rich-quick business. Although it is the most surefire way to wealth, it is quite the opposite of getting rich quick. It is a slow and steady process.

Your first or next investment should fall under one of two buying strategies. You will want to acquire a home either by using a lease option or by using some form of a conventional method. You may want to use a Realtor to help find a home and a mortgage broker to help with a loan to finance it. You will want to pick one of these two options and forget about everything else until you get your next property. The most successful people in the world stay focused, so I encourage you to focus on one strategy to get going.

Lease Options

We have already gone through the basics of the lease option. It is really simple; you will want to lease the property from the owners for five years or more with an option to buy. You will then either sublease or sublease with an option with your tenants, otherwise known as a rent to own. You have seen examples and understand the huge profit potential with this buying strategy.

The Paperwork

Most people, including myself, want to understand all the paperwork before they ever pick up the phone to call anyone. A word of caution: do not let being scared of paperwork, or anything else for that matter, stop you from moving forward. That being said, let's talk about the paperwork so that you can get a good grasp of it. In the appendix of this book, you will see samples of all the actual documents I use in my investing.

Paperwork to Use with the Seller

- ***Seller Call Sheet***

You will want to stay as organized as you can, so you will want a way to handle your leads. I use what I call a Seller Call Sheet. This sheet is very important to me because I can track where the lead came from, and I can gather all the information at once. It helps me remember everything. Complete it the best you can. Some questions on there will really draw out motivation, like "When are you moving?" and "What if the house does not sell?"

- ***Lease Purchase Agreement***

This document will spell out the terms that you and the seller agree to. You will always want the lease with the right to buy in one contract. Once you have this signed by the seller, you have the deal "locked up." This is one of the most important documents in your arsenal. I have included a blank sample along with a completed sample in the appendix. Below, I have given explanations of the sections in the contract.

Section 1. The contract needs to have the seller/landlord names, the buyer/tenant names, the property address, and the date.

Section 2. The next section of the contract is the lease. It spells out the monthly payments, when the payments will start, how much of each payment is applied to the purchase, and the length of the lease. My agreement is set up to be a one-year lease that automatically renews every year that I don't cancel.

Section 3. This is the option to buy. You can read the agreement, but you will see that it spells out the price, how the money will be paid, and the current liens.

Section 4. The final section is all the provisions. Let's go through these one by one.

Utilities. This one is easy. You, the tenant/buyer, will pay all utilities. The sellers are happy about this, and remember, you require your tenant to pay these anyway.

Maintenance. You can do whatever you want here. If the seller really wants me to take care of all maintenance, and I agree to that, I simply put $1,000 here. Anything above that should be covered by the insurance, so that is how I would explain it to the seller. I normally use $200 here.

Title. You will need some additional paperwork signed at another meeting with the seller. I will go over when and how all that works. This provision just states that other paperwork is needed later. Similar to an actual closing.

Inspection. This is an easy way out and just a warm fuzzy for you. It is not even important that this clause be here, but you can get out of the deal if you change your mind later, because you have not approved the property in writing.

Assignment. This states that you will be subleasing the property without the seller's permission. The seller knows this up front. This also allows you to sell your contract to another investor without the seller's permission. This is beyond the scope of this book, but if you get a great deal on a lease option, you can sell your deal to someone else for a quick profit because of this clause.

Access. You need access immediately to start showing the property to prospective tenants or to do anything you need in order to get the property ready. Always get a key when the seller signs this agreement.

Illegal provision. You can use this agreement in any state because of this clause. We don't want to violate any state laws. This clause is very common in legal documents.

Insurance. This one is very, very important. It states that you will be added to the insurance policy and that if there are damages, it is the seller's responsibility to make the repairs. It also states that you will not be making payments on a house that is in need of the repairs. I have used this one on a property that was flooded from a broken pipe. The damages were not repaired for three months. I stopped making payments on the deal until the house was ready to re-rent, and the seller did not have a problem with it.

Qualified resident. I sometimes use this one and sometimes take it out. Some sellers hate it. Other investors will tell you to always use this clause, and honestly, it is not a bad idea. I, however, normally write my agreements so that I don't make a payment until I find someone, so I don't feel this clause is necessary on those deals.

- **Addendum A: Lease Purchase Agreement**

Use this form for anything else you agree to that cannot fit on the normal form. For example, if I negotiated that my payment will increase after five years, I would use this form. This type of agreement would read something like this: "Tenant's monthly payment will increase $50 per month beginning on February 1, 2020."

It is common for me to use the form to spell out a purchase price. For example, if there was very little equity in the home, I might negotiate a price of the balance of the loan. That way each time I make a payment, the purchase price is reduced on all amortized loans. The seller is normally receptive to this, so it is easy to get and can add a tremendous amount of profit on longer-term agreements.

- **Option Affidavit**

This is one of two forms you will record at the county. This form "clouds the title." Clouding the title simply means making it so the seller cannot transfer clean title. If the title transfers, you can sue the seller, indicating that you had the option to buy the home. This type of lawsuit would be settled by the title insurer. For this reason, title insurance companies will not insure a title that is clouded, and lenders require title insurance, so it would be very difficult for anyone to get a loan against the property. This is one way I protect myself from the seller taking out a loan or selling the home without me knowing about it.

You will complete the Option Affidavit with the seller's name as it appears on the title and the legal address. It does not disclose any information about the deal because your deal is nobody else's business. It simply notifies the public that you have an interest in the property. You will want to either mail or hand-deliver this to the county recorder. There is a fee to record something, so check with your county before you mail it.

You can always just have the lease purchase contract notarized and record it. It will also cloud the title, but by recording the lease purchase contract, you are telling the world about the details of your agreement. Typically, you want to keep the details private, which is why I recommend the Option Affidavit.

- ### *Deed of Trust/Mortgage*
This is a lien. When you buy a home and sign a note, you will also sign a deed of trust or mortgage to secure the note. This document spells out all the requirements of the seller, including keeping the insurance and taxes paid, etc. The Option Affidavit is good and works most of the time; this document should work every time. In fact, when you buy the home, you will need to sign a release of this lien. Don't worry about that, because the title company will handle it.

I did not include this form in the appendix. I have had multiple opinions on the actual language in my document, so I would much rather see you have your own attorney draft this document for you. The disagreement between attorneys and title companies is in the language, not the fact that I use it. All good attorneys agree that this document should be used.

- ### *Addition Insured Letter*
Remember I mentioned being added to the insurance policy? The mortgage companies have interest in the property and are added, so why don't we? We can and should. It does not cost anything and is really easy to do. Have the seller sign this letter and provide you with the agent's name and number. You will just call the agent and let him or her know you

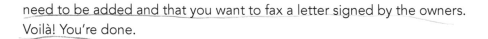

need to be added and that you want to fax a letter signed by the owners. Voilà! You're done.

- **Sales Contract**

This is probably not necessary, but I like the seller to sign another contract that actually spells out the entire purchase transaction. The contract will have an "on or before" closing date. This date is the same as the expiration of your option. You will keep this contract in your files, and it is just one more way to be sure the seller performs on the agreement.

- **Authorization to Release Information**

This form allows you to talk to the seller's mortgage company.

- **Direct-Payments Authorization**

Sometimes I make my monthly payments directly to the seller's mortgage company, and sometimes I make it to the seller. If I make a payment to the seller, I want to be sure he or she makes the payments. This form states that if the seller doesn't make the payments, you can. It also states that if he or she falls behind, you will be credited three dollars for every one dollar you spend to bring the loan current. This works great if the seller has equity. If not, it is safer for you to make the payment directly to the mortgage company, in which case you may choose not to use this form.

Paperwork to Use with the Tenant

- **Resident Call Sheet**

I call this the Buyer Call Sheet, but I am referring to either tenants or tenant buyers. This is basically the same as the Seller Call Sheet. I want to know as much as possible about them up front, and I want to know where the calls are coming from so I know what marketing is working. You will go through a lot of these forms because you will get a lot of these types of calls. Do your best to fill out a form for each potential tenant.

- **Application**

I keep a stack of these in the house. You can add or take away questions that you feel are or are not important to know. You need a name, address, social security number, and birth date to run credit and criminal background checks. You also want to keep your application simple, because you want tenants to complete it on the initial appointment. Once they go home, they may change their minds, but once they complete an application, they may feel committed. There is a balance here, because a good application helps with the screening and will help with debt collection if you ever need to resort to that.

Here are a few of the most important things to ask, in my opinion:

Current monthly rent or house payment. I don't want their new payment to be more than 120 percent of what they are currently paying. I have found with a large payment increase, a default is more likely.

Length of desired occupancy. I am not interested in anything less than a year.

Past two former addresses. I want this even if they have been at the current address for several years. I want to call both places, because sometimes the current landlord will give a good reference just to get rid of them. The prior landlord has no reason to lie.

Emergency contact. An emergency to me is not paying rent. I want to know whom I can call.

Tools you own. I want to make sure they know they need to mow the yard, remove the snow, and vacuum the carpet.

- ***Deposit Receipt***
This states that the tenant is giving you a deposit to hold the home for him or her. I try not to accept less than one month's payment. Always try to get a deposit up front. If you deny the application for whatever reason, you can give the deposit back. It is nonrefundable if a tenant changes his or her mind. This really gets the tenant committed and excited about the home.

- ***Rental Agreement/Lease***
My lease is 100 percent in my favor. It pretty much gives the tenant no rights, and that's how I want it. I know I am an honest person and will not screw someone, but I cannot say the same about the tenants. I demand no wiggle room with this agreement.

I actually use a different lease with my tenant buyer than with my tenants. Let me first go through some of the important clauses you need to have in your lease, and then I will go through the differences between the two that I use.

Rent amount. Be sure you have a late fee and a returned-check fee. Some landlords like a daily late fee, which I would only recommend if you have an office. Because most of my tenants mail the rent, I do not charge a daily late fee. I ran into issues with them blaming the postal service for a few extra days, which is never a fun conversation to have. There is no arguing a flat fee. I start my evictions very fast, so I price my late fee high enough that if it takes a few extra days, I am still come out ahead.

Delivery of rent. If you work out of your home, you will want tenants to meet you somewhere and bring the rent. Before I had an office, I would not allow that. My tenants had just a few options, one of them being me coming out to get the rent for a fee, but no option allowed them to come to me. While we are on the topic, be sure to get a post office box if you don't have an office. You do not want any of your tenants to know where you live if you can avoid it.

Maintenance. I want all maintenance requests in excess of $50 in writing. It has never happened, but if I were to get sued for not fixing something that I was unaware of, I would argue that I never received a written request and that my lease demands it. In the appendix, the lease states that the tenant is responsible for the first $200 in repairs. I use this lease for my rent-to-own tenants. You can cut this part out of the lease for a normal tenant or for a tenant buyer and say that the tenant is responsible for all maintenance.

Re-rent access and fee. I have made more money on this one clause than any other clause in my lease. It is a fee for the tenant to break the lease. Whenever you evict or the tenant stops paying, you can ask for this fee. You may not be able to collect it, but it is something you can add when you send the tenant to collections.

Liability. I had a tenant ask that I replace a CD player she stored under the kitchen sink because the sink started to leak, and the player was damaged. Are you kidding me? Why the heck did you store your CD player under the kitchen sink? Sorry…I just get emotional about this one. This clause protects you against any damage to your tenants' personal belongings. It is important that you have no liability, and it is a good idea to have them get their own insurance to protect their property.

There are a few important differences between the tenant lease and the tenant-buyer lease.

1. The tenant lease automatically rolls to a month-to-month. I like this because I don't need to worry about a renewal, and it gives me the option to raise the rents. I love making it roll to a month-to-month, but if you wanted to renew the tenant, it would be a great time to visit your property.

2. The tenant-buyer lease expires because it has to, but it does have an automatic rent increase built in. It is easy to tell your tenant about the rent increase because it is normally how you do your deals, and it is on the lease. Taxes and insurance go up with the rest of inflation, so should rent.

3. The tenant lease says that the landlord is not responsible for any drain blockage of any kind. I bold this so tenants know without a doubt that I am not paying for this no matter what caused it. If somehow the sewer line collapsed, I would probably pay for that, but I am not paying for my plumber to remove toys from the toilet.

4. The tenant-buyer lease says the tenant is responsible for all maintenance.

• **Option**

Notice how the lease and option are two separate forms for your tenants. You also want the option to become null and void if any part of the lease is broken. This works so that you can evict the tenant in the case of a default. If the lease and option were on one form, the judge would see the option and might consider the tenant as having equitable interest in the home. That is a legal term, and it's not necessary that you know what it means. What is important to understand is that if you give someone equitable interest, you could have just sold him or her the home. This will cause additional risk for you, so you should avoid this whenever possible. Some of the risks to giving up equitable interest in the home include the following:

- There may be licensing requirements to do this.
- Additional disclosure may be necessary.
- The terms you can charge could be restrictive.
- Foreclosure could be tougher.

Using separate option and lease forms does not always protect against giving up equitable interest, but it definitely helps. This is one of the main reasons I suggest you run your business plan and documents past a real estate attorney.

Another important thing to point out about the option is that you will be transferring the property in "as is" condition and that the recording of the option will void it. Remember we talked about recording the Option Affidavit when buying to cloud the title? What do you think will happen if your tenant buyer records the option? The last thing is hidden in clause 9, but you want to be sure that you cannot be sued if your seller defaults. Because you don't own the home yet, you cannot sell it. If your seller defaults and you don't buy the home, you can get sued for not performing. This clause says that you may or may not be the owner, and if for any reason you cannot perform, you will refund the option payment and void the agreement. I have never run into a problem where I had to use this and pray I never do. I also have never had a tenant buyer question it.

- **Move-In Checklist**

Give tenants two copies, one for them to keep and one to return to you. You will also want them to sign a receipt that they received the two copies. This is more to protect them from your keeping their deposit for damage that was already there. At least that is what you tell them, and you are not lying, because it does protect them. More important to us, however, is that you can charge them for their damages, and they cannot argue that the damage was already there. Most of the time, you will never get the checklist back from them. In this case, everything must have been in working order. The acceptance clause in the lease states that the tenant agrees that everything is in working order if the checklist is not returned within seven days, so if you never get the checklist returned, everything was in working order.

add it!

- **Third-Party Forms**

Some utility providers will allow you to be notified if there are any missed payments on your tenant's bills. This is a great indication if the tenant is starting to struggle or if the tenant has vacated the house, especially if the rent payments are coming from an outside source like the tenant's employer or government assistance. Oftentimes the utility company will require written permission from the tenant, so this is something I have the tenant sign up front.

Generate Leads (Lots of Them)

The key to being successful in any sales position—which is what this is—is to have plenty of leads. With a high number of leads, you can mess one up and not get down on yourself. It is kind of like diversifying in the stock market; if one stock crashes, you have others working. This also makes it less likely that you will get involved in a bad deal just to have a deal.

Throughout your career, you will learn hundreds of ways to generate prospects. In the beginning, I want you to focus on three. To have the highest level of success, I recommend you do not veer outside of these three lead-generating sources until you have them mastered. Then and only then is it OK to add another lead-generating vehicle.

The three things you will focus on are outbound calls, signs, and networking.

Outbound Calls

Outbound calls sound dreadful and scary. Let's call it tele-money, dialing for dollars, or calling for cash, because that's really what it is. The phone is the single highest-paying tool in our office. The more calls we make, the more money we make; it's that simple.

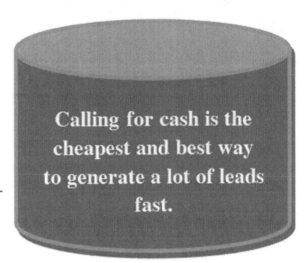

Calling for cash is the cheapest and best way to generate a lot of leads fast.

The only reason to use the phone is to find people open to talking to you about your ideas. Notice I said "open to talking" and not "wanting to sell you their house over the phone." In order to sell your ideas, you will want to set an appointment and meet them in person. Over time you will become more selective about the people you meet, but in the beginning your main goal should be meeting with people and not necessarily buying houses. For this reason, you want to set lots of appointments and get lots of practice. Trust me; you will end up with houses as you practice your selling and negotiating skills.

You will have better luck with FRBO (For Rent by Owner) ads than you will with FSBO (For Sale by Owner) ads. If you are strapped for time, I suggest you focus on FRBOs. However, time permitting, call both.

When you call the owner, it is OK to sound nervous. In fact it is good, because if you sound professional, you are less likely to make progress. Sellers are sometimes intimidated by professionals. I think they fear being taken advantage of.

Please refer to the Lease Option FRBO Phone Script in the appendix. There are a few parts of this script that I want to mention. At the time of the call, you really don't care about the house. What you are looking for is a situation. You want to find a seller who is motivated to sell and willing to sell on your terms. The features of the house mean nothing until you start negotiating the deal. It is, however, important to get the seller talking about the house, because to the seller, it is all about the house.

When you ask people to tell you about their house, sometimes landlords or sellers will say, "What do you want to know?" Don't panic when they say this. Simply do what you can to get them talking about the house. The best way is to say something like, "Oh, I don't know," and ask a question about it. One of my favorites is "What is your favorite feature?"

Don't encourage them to talk too long. You want to get on and off the phone fast so you can make a lot of calls. If necessary, interrupt them with respect to keep their description of the house to a minute or two.

For the FRBOs, your next goal is to interest them in a long lease. I suggest two years because although it is longer than normal, it is not so long that they will immediately say no. You will never do a deal for only two years, but this is an easy way to find out if they are open to a long-term lease. If they say no to two years, you know they will say no to five years or more.

The next goal is to find out if they want to—or are at least open to—the idea of selling. This is where you will weed out most of your prospects. Most will say no, which is OK, because some will say yes. If they say no, get off the phone as quickly as possible so you can continue making calls. You can say, "OK, I am really interested in buying a home, so this one will not fit my needs. Thank you," and hang up. Do not even give them a chance to respond. It may sound rude, but it really isn't. What is rude is taking your time and theirs on a deal that will never happen.

After you know they will sell, you want to let them know you are an investor. You can simply tell them, but I think it is easier to do it the way the script describes. If you ask a question immediately after telling them, they will answer the question instead of questioning you about being an investor. You want them to know, because when you meet with them, you will be letting them know you will not be living in the home. If they don't know you are an investor, it could be a huge surprise. They may not be willing to work with an investor, so again, you may be wasting your time by meeting with them.

If owners do question you about being an investor, your response is, "I know you probably have heard a lot of really bad things about investors and that investors are out there trying to steal homes. You probably would never even consider accepting an offer from an investor even if it was fair, would you?" They most likely will say yes, they would consider an offer. If they say they would not, which has happened on occasion, this is good to know as soon as possible. You can smile and move on.

but I will make a fair offer based on mkt. value

As soon as the appointment is set, be sure to ask if the person you are talking to is the owner. Trust me; you will learn the hard way if you don't ask. I have been on more appointments than I can count with someone who couldn't make decisions. You really want to be sure all decision makers are there for the appointment.

Once you start feeling confident in the home, you will want to further qualify prospects on the phone. You will want to start by asking them why they are selling. Listen very carefully to their answer. If they say anything about not being sure they want to sell, or if they say for the right offer they are willing to sell, cancel the appointment because they are not motivated. If they say a reason that screams motivation, like they never wanted the house in the first place, or they are only renting it because they can't afford payments on a vacant house, you are more likely to make a deal with them.

If they are not motivated, you will simply call them back before the appointment to cancel. You can say you found another home you are considering. This will not be a lie because you will always be looking at other homes.

The FSBO is a much easier script because you already know owners are willing to sell. Set an appointment if you receive an answer you like when you ask why they are selling. Do not try to sell your ideas on the phone! Another question to consider is asking if they are living in the home and if they have found another home yet. From here you can find out their time-line for selling and whether or not they need the money from one home to move into another.

Unless the prop. is too far...

Making the Calls

The best way to make your calls is to get the classified section of the news-paper and open to the For Rent section. Go through the ads and cross out all those that look like a management company. You will know it is a management company because they are required to disclose this in the ad. Normally, you will see three initials before the phone number or the name of the company spelled out.

> 987 W 100th Cir, $1275 3bd, 2ba, bsmt, yrd, gar, wd, fp, sec 8 ok, no smk CMA (303) 123-4567

Sample ad from a Property
Management Company

Once you have crossed out the ads you will not call, go to the areas clos-est to your home and start calling. Call every single ad that you did not cross out. Do not even look at or read the ad; just call the number. It may be helpful to start at the bottom of a column and work your way up. You will be wasting time if you start to read and look for the perfect prop-erty. Remember, we are looking for a situation that needs our help, not a property.

I also recommend you have a follow-up system or a tickler file. The file I used was one of those accordion files that had 31 pockets, one for each day of the month. I completed a Seller Call Sheet for each contact I made. If I did not set the appointment and sensed a hint of motivation, I stuck the paper in the accordion file for a few days later. Each day

I made calls, I pulled out all the sheets for that day and made those calls first. If I left a message or did not get an appointment, I would move the sheet down about a week and follow up again. After several calls, I would also start sending letters. Use a similar system for all appointments you go on. If there is any sense of motivation, keep calling them until they either work with you or get their problem solved somewhere else. Trust me, they will not be upset with you calling and checking in because, although you may not be viewed as the best option, you are an option nonetheless.

If time permits, you may want to drive through neighborhoods you are interested in and look for FSBO and FRBO signs. Some inexperienced landlords will buy tiny signs at the hardware store that nobody can read. This may be the only advertising they are doing, so you may be the only call they receive, and you could appear as their only option.

Finally, spend some time on the Internet. Many landlords are moving away from advertising in papers and are advertising on sites such as craigslist. org and rentals.com. There are many other sites that allow FSBO and FRBO advertising, so do a search on Google, Bing, or Yahoo! and find some of your favorites to use.

You might find it easier to compile a list of phone numbers before you start making calls. With Craigslist especially, I have found that many landlords and sellers post ads in multiple days and sections, so I end up calling the same person multiple times. You can eliminate or reduce this if you make a list first.

If you are short on time, you can age your list. If you call two or more weeks after you create your list, many people would have already rented or sold their house. The ones who have not could be more motivated to listen to options. This should speed up your process of talking to people you can help.

Like I mentioned earlier, your goal in the beginning is to set appointments so you can get in the house and practice. Make no mistake—there is a learning curve here, and you want that curve to be as short as possible so you can start making money. In my experience, 95 percent of successful investors start here. Do not skip this step, no matter how uncomfortable or scary it is. These calls are *that* important. Go practice!

Deborah

Steph and I were calling around 50 people every weekend. Finally, we reached Deborah, a motivated seller. Deborah was a tired landlord and had two of her 12 units vacant. She no longer wanted to be a landlord because the recent vacancies were expensive and ate up her reserves. We found her through an FRBO ad. Not having much in the way of reserves, the vacancies were really killing her, and she thought she might miss a mortgage payment. It took us well over 200 phone calls to find Deborah. At that time in our careers, we were trying to sell our ideas on the phone, making us much less effective.

I told Deborah everything about what we wanted to offer, including price and payments. She thought it was a good idea but wanted us to view the home. She had her daughter and her daughter's boyfriend meet us at the property. After viewing the home, we decided we wanted to do a deal.

Deborah really needed the vacancy problem fixed, and we really wanted our first creative deal, so we agreed to a four-year term, a monthly payment of $1,400, which is what we could rent it for, and a price of $195,000, which was the value at the time.

Not a good deal, right? We paid full price and market rent, and to make things worse, we gave her $2,000 up front. Of course we did a cash advance on a credit card to get the $2,000. Actually, it was a great deal—because it was our first deal.

We had ordered the contracts from the Internet. Once we had them signed and had the keys, we started cleaning the place up. We did not do much except remove some dated wallpaper and paint the walls. We quickly started a marketing campaign to locate a tenant. We'd learned that selling a home as a rent to own would demand a higher rent and would be easier to manage, so we offered our new investment as a rent to own. We found a tenant within a few weeks. We collected $3,000 down from our new tenant with a monthly rent amount of $1,400 and a purchase price of $230,000 within two years. That person ended up moving out, and we found a new tenant. The new tenant also moved out, and we ended up giving the property back to Deborah at the end of the term. We did not lose any money when the whole thing was done, and we gained an awful lot of experience.

The first deal does not need to be perfect; it just needs to get done.

Signs

Depending on your budget, you can either have these professionally made or you can hand make them. Either way will work about the same. Using a professional will save you a bunch of time and will not be very expensive.

The message is important, so put some thought into it. Many people will use signs that say "We Buy Houses" or "Avoid Foreclosure." There are many other messages you can use. "We Buy Homes" and our number worked the best for us. I like to keep it simple, and there is no question what we do. Don't you hate when you see advertising and have no idea what product or service is being offered?

We started with poster board, but I strongly recommend you use a higher-quality product. Corrugated plastic really is the most common material used and for good reason. It is cheap and durable, and the plastic works so much better than the poster board because it can't be damaged in the weather. You can do a search on the Internet for these signs. You will want to buy a large staple gun to attach these to poles, or you could use stakes in the ground. One of my favorite ways to hang these is on a wood stake I put in the ground. You simply hammer in the stake and then staple the sign to the stake. Hang your signs at large intersections where a lot of cars stop for red lights. My highest success has come from interstate off-ramps.

To have success, you want to be consistent. Put up at least 10 every week. You may want to rotate between two to four areas. Keep hitting the same areas so people living nearby see the signs over and over. In marketing, it takes someone seeing your message seven times on average before the person will call. If you are not consistent, don't even waste your money buying the signs.

You will notice that builders and politicians use these signs a lot. The builders will often put them up on a Friday and take them down on a Sunday evening. If you are concerned about getting into any trouble or if it makes you feel more comfortable, leave them up for the weekend and take them down.

When you get a call from a seller, use the Seller Phone Script found in the appendix.

Ralph and Yolanda

Shortly after finding the first tenant for Deborah's property, we started hanging corrugated plastic signs on the side of the road. The signs read "We Buy Homes" and included our phone number. We also hung the signs as high as we could to keep them out of the reach of children. These signs are often referred to as "bandit signs" because you are not really supposed to hang them. Steph and I would go out late at night to put up our signs. We would dress in all black and call ourselves "ninjas of the night" in jest, but we did go out at night when there was less traffic. We figured if we got fined, we could chalk it up to a cost of doing business. Just to be clear, in our entire career, the worst that ever happened was a code-enforcement officer noticed us hanging some signs and asked that we take them down. We have never received a fine. You may get threatening phone calls, but for the most part, these are harmless. I justified using the signs because I was buying properties in the area and managing them well. I was increasing the rental rates and values in the area, so the eyesore of my sign was justified by what I was doing for the neighborhood.

These signs flat out work. Later in our careers, we started tracking all our marketing efforts and tracked both the quality and the cost of the calls. We used everything from door hangers, direct mail, newspaper ads, radio ads, and bandit signs. Bandit signs were hands down the most cost-effective, even when we were paying someone else to put them up for us.

Ralph called us from one of our signs. He said he needed to sell his house fast because he had another one built, and he and his family were moving. Knowing that they were having trouble selling their home and that they were now forced to make two house payments, I set an appointment to meet with him and his wife, Yolanda.

We got to the home and looked around before sitting down. Not knowing much about selling, we dove right into the numbers like we did for all our appointments. We did everything wrong with our negotiating, but they were so motivated, it did not matter. They were determined to work with us. These are the kinds of sellers we are looking for!

We were a little smarter after our experience with Deborah and put nothing down, but again, we agreed to start making payments immediately and paid full price and full market rent. I guess we still needed practice.

The terms looked like this: We signed a lease option with a four-year term, $1,300 a month, and a price of $175,000. By placing ads in the local papers, we found our first tenant. We offered it on a rent to own for a $3,000 option payment, $1,395 per month, and a price of $200,000.

Agreement with Seller		Agreement with Tenant/Buyer	
Option Payment	$ -	Option Payment	$3,000.00
Monthly Payment	$1,300.00	Monthly Payment	$1,395.00
Purchase Price	$175,000.00	Purchase Price	$200,000.00
Term	48 Months	Term	24 Months

Profit:

Option money:	$3,000
24-month cash flow:	$2,280
Purchase spread:	$22,000 (remember, the $3,000 option money is applied to the purchase)

Not so bad for stumbling through it and doing a far-from-perfect job negotiating!

Networking

I have had several deals come to me because friends, family, and other people knew what we did. If everyone who knows you knows what you do, they will tell others. Go to events like meetings, seminars, and leads groups. This takes a while to build, and it actually never ends, but as more and more people learn what you do, you will see more and more referrals.

Referrals are the best leads you can get. For one, they are free. Free is good. Also, they are normally higher quality because they already know what you do and probably already trust you.

One of the first things you want to do is order business cards. Don't print these on your computer at home. Be sure to pay a professional printer to do them for you. Your card is a direct reflection of you, so you want them to be nice. I recommend using both sides of the card as well, giving people enough information so that there is no doubt what you do or whom you are trying to help. On the back of your card, you can list the common situations that lease options help solve. For example, if you are focused on lease options, you are not in the ugly-house business, so your card might not say "foreclosure" or "buy as is" or any other phrase that indicates you buy beat-up homes. Here are some ideas:

- Bad tenants?
- Double payments?
- Job transfer?
- Little or no equity?

You have probably noticed that all professional athletes have routines. They do the same things over and over and over. Think about Tiger Woods or other professional golfers. Every time they come to the tee they do the same thing. Why? It is their system for success. Real estate should be no different. You must have a system to use every time you meet with a seller. Find something that works and do it over and over and over.

Remember: focus on one niche. If you are looking for lease options, do not advertise yourself as a foreclosure expert.

Think of it this way. If you need heart surgery, would you go to a general practitioner? Probably not. You will want help from someone who specializes in your problem.

Tell everyone you know that you are a real estate investor looking for nice homes with little to no equity.

I would do a lot of online networking in real estate forums. This worked best for me by answering questions or starting discussions that were of value. I logged in each day to see how I could contribute and get my name out there. When appropriate, I let people know that I was looking for deals.

We had several deals under our belt when I met Keith. He stumbled onto the site looking for an investor to buy a fourplex he owned. He and I quickly connected, and we did a no-money-down lease option on the building. This turned out to be a great deal, but what made it even better is that he had two other properties that we eventually took over. All three properties have positive cash flow, and Keith and I have become friends.

What to Say in the House

You will want to study this section of the book. This could be the most important section you read. You will want to reread and practice before you ever go on an appointment. Practice during the appointments and keep getting better. Aside from marketing, this will be your highest-paid skill as an investor. Steph and I practiced with each other. We would role-play the different things that could happen in the house. If you don't have someone to role-play with, use a mirror, a pet, or anything you can find. The point is, you need to *practice*!

When studying selling, you will learn a five-step process. It is no different with real estate. The key to your success will be doing the same thing over and over. Become a master. If you vary from the five-step system, you will not reach your potential. These are the five steps.

1. Make a friend.
2. Get a commitment.
3. Do a motivation/needs analysis.
4. Settle financials.
5. Make the offer.

Make a Friend

You may have heard this referred to as the five-minute friend because you need to make a friend in the first five minutes. The goal of this step is to start building rapport. It is simple to do in real estate because you will be spending a little time with the seller as you walk through the home.

When you first meet at the door, be sure to smile and say hello. Once inside, ask the seller to show you around. It is not important that a husband/ wife combo walk around with you, but it is important that you get at least one of the owners to walk around with you. If the seller suggests you just walk around, put pressure on him or her to walk you around.

You can say something like, "Well, I may have some questions; do you mind giving me a quick tour?"

During your tour, be sure to ask open-ended questions that get the owners talking about themselves, and then do your best to relate. The tour is not really to look at the house—although you are doing that—the tour is used to build rapport. People only do business with people they like and trust. Many successful sales trainers will tell you that if you can remember FORM, (Friends, Occupation, Recreation, Message) you will be a friend-finding machine.

F	Friends and Family
O	Occupation
R	Recreation
M	Message

Go through each letter in the acronym. Ask questions to get them talking about themselves. Notice that your message is last. Make friends before you talk business. Look at a picture on the wall and ask about it.

"Are these friends of yours?" or "Is this you and your family on vacation?"

Ask if they have kids or grandkids. Ask what they do for a living or what they do for fun. If they say something you both have in common, be sure to let them know. People love to talk about themselves, and you can become one of their best friends if you just let them do it. People also like others who are similar to them, so if you can relate to anything, do.

Get a Commitment

Once you have seen the house, ask them where they would like to sit down and talk. Most of the time it will be at the kitchen table, but sometimes it will be in the living room. I have heard several different opinions about where you should sit, at what point you should sit, how you sit, etc. If you ask me, it is all a bunch of nonsense. I think it is easy to just ask them where you should sit. Sometimes you will be looking at a vacant house, in which case you can simply ask where would be a good place to talk. You want them to be comfortable, so let them tell you where you will be talking.

Once you sit down, your first goal is to be open with them and get their commitment that they will be open and honest with you. Either a "yes" or a "no" is fine, but make sure they know that you are looking for a decision. There are several ways to do this; I am going to explain what I feel works best.

When I sit down, I will use the seller's name and say something like this:

YOU: Mr. Seller, I am here to talk to you about your house and to see if there is a way I can help you. You understand that this is a business for me, and in order for me to get involved, I need to be able to make a profit, right?

SELLER: Yes, of course.

You: We are going to spend a little time together, and I will do the best I can to make you an offer that meets your needs and makes me a profit, and I really need your help. Can you promise to be honest and tell me if you hate my ideas? Sometimes my ideas are really crazy, and you won't hurt my feelings.

Seller: Yes. (Of course he or she is going to say yes.)

You: Great! I promise to tell you today if I feel I can meet your needs and still make a profit. After our discussion, can you promise to tell me if you feel I can meet your needs or if you feel my ideas are way too crazy for you?

Seller: Sure, I can do that.

You: Just so we are clear, I am promising to tell you either yes, I feel we can work together, or no, I don't think this will work. I am promising to do this before we are finished today. Can I expect the same courtesy in return?

Seller: I said yes.

There you have it. The seller won't always follow through with his or her promise, but you have just gotten him or her to commit to telling you yes or no. A "no" is OK, and a "yes" is great, but a "maybe" will drive you crazy and will waste your time.

You can say it however you want, but be sure it is clear that you are an investor and you need to make a profit to get involved. Sellers are not idiots. They know you are there to make money, but telling them this will help them relax. They won't feel like you are trying to pull a fast one or hide anything. Who is not going to agree to extend you courtesy when you took the time to come listen to his or her problem?

Motivation/Needs Analysis

One of the most important lessons you will ever learn in selling is to have a really good understanding of someone's needs *before* you try selling that person anything. Always, always, always talk about his or her needs and draw out his or her motivation *before* you talk about money or what you have to offer. From our earlier examples, you can see that you will still get deals by not following this advice, but please learn from our mistakes to maximize success.

It sounds bad, but you need to bring out all the seller's motivation. The more emotional it gets, the better it is, because these are issues the seller needs to face. You are there to help, but you need him or her to understand the seriousness of the issues. Several times we have had sellers break down and cry. There is some serious motivation when you see this!

After I get my commitment, I transition to motivation by asking, "What were you hoping I could do for you today?"

The seller will almost always laugh and say, "Buy my house."

Your response should *always* be, "Well, what else have you tried?"

You will want to spend no less than 30 minutes with the seller talking about what he or she has tried or thought about trying. Ask more and more questions, and get the seller talking about his or her situation. You will also want to use negative phrases, saying things that you know are not true but saying them in a way that makes them seem to be true.

An example for someone who can't afford two payments could be: "Well, at least you have time to wait for a really attractive offer." The seller will quickly tell you how wrong you are. It is a great technique to make the person tell you something you already know. It is always best if the seller says what is bothering him or her and tells you why he or she is motivated. Here are some examples of common situations and the kinds of questions or statements I would use:

If the seller is falling behind on payments due to losing his or her job:

"I heard the job market is really good right now. You should have no problem finding another job."

"I am sure you are not too worried. I mean, you will probably find a job that pays you even more than you were making."

"At least you got a great severance package and can afford to stay here if you wanted."

"You are probably getting several calls a day from people with job offers, right?"

If the seller is falling behind because of a divorce:

"I heard there are a lot of divorces where the wife and the husband really got along and there were no issues with dividing assets."

"How has your ex-husband been to work with?"

"The good thing is that your ex-wife is helping you with the mortgage payments, right?"

"At least you and your ex-wife are parting on great terms."

If the seller's house was trashed by the last tenant:

"The good thing is, this was probably the first time you ever had that kind of tenant."

"Tell me a little about how the tenant was to work with."

"What was the tenant's reason for doing what he/she did?"

If the seller just got a job transfer:

"At least you can afford to make payments on two houses with your big raise."

"How much help is your company giving you with selling your home here?"

"You can probably rent the house. I mean, it would not be that hard to manage it from Chicago."

Some of this sounds funny, and it is. These are things I actually say to people in these situations. I cannot express enough how important it is for the seller to tell you his or her problems. Once you get all the person's problems out in the open, two things will happen. First, the seller loves you because you listened, and second, the seller wants to hear how you can help him or her.

Many sellers will want to talk about the money and what you can offer from the start. Do not let them control the meeting. Only talk about money after you have gone through needs analysis and discovered their motivation.

Financials

Before you can make an offer, you need to know the financials in order to structure a win-win deal. This includes everything about the seller's mortgage, taxes, and insurance, how much he or she thinks it would rent or sell for, and anything else you think you will need to know. By the time you get to this step, there should be no hesitation by the seller. In fact, you may have received most of this information through your other questions, but you will want to go over it again. You can plant more seeds here by saying things to remind the seller of the payment and affirm that it is not easy to make the payments. For example, when he or she tells you how much the payment is, you can and should say, "Well the good thing is, you can make those payments on the empty house for six or more months while you are waiting for it to sell."

Make Your Offer

Finally, you are ready to make an offer. As you get more tools in your investor's tool belt, you will have more options. For now I would focus on offering a lease option.

During your offer, avoid real estate jargon. You do not want to confuse the seller, and even if he or she knows what you are talking about, you do not want to sound too smart. If you were a seller, would you rather sell your home to someone smarter than you or someone not as smart as you? It is OK to sound a little on the "slow" side while you are making offers and negotiating deals. I try to avoid the words "lease" or "options." I replace them with words or phrases such as "rent" or "cashing you out." To me that is easier for everyone to understand and get excited about.

Before you make an offer, say, "What if..." Simply using the words "what if" before your offer gets the seller fully committed (verbally, of course) before you ever say you can do anything. I also like to say, "You probably hate this idea, and there is probably no way this will work, but what if... blah, blah, blah."

Don't go for the close right away. Make your offer and then ask, "Is this something we should even talk about?" Getting the seller to agree to discuss it is a baby step that most sellers will say yes to. Once he or she says yes, ask what is it about the offer the seller likes or what about the offer will solve his or her problem. This gets the seller talking about the offer, making it seem like his or her idea, and the seller literally starts talking himself or herself into it. This is so much fun. You can actually start saying things like, "I am not sure that will work for me. Why do you think it is a good deal for everyone?" and the seller will start trying to sell you on the idea. Some sellers will beg you to buy the house. It may seem hard to do at first, but I encourage you to make your offers this way.

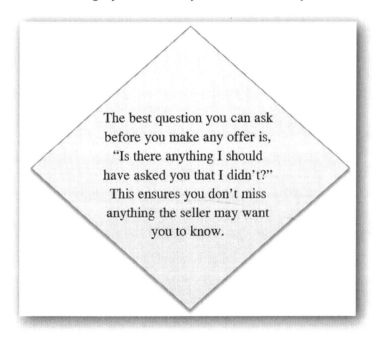

The best question you can ask before you make any offer is, "Is there anything I should have asked you that I didn't?" This ensures you don't miss anything the seller may want you to know.

You: OK, I think I understand the situation, and we went over all your financials. Is there anything I should have asked that I didn't?

SELLER: No, you did a great job.

YOU: Now, I am not sure I can do this. You probably already hate the idea, and there is probably no way this will work, but what if I guarantee you a monthly payment for a set amount of time? I will take care of all the day-to-day maintenance, and then at some point down the road, I cash you out, giving you close to what you are asking. Is that something we should even talk about or probably not?

SELLER: Sure, we can talk about it.

YOU: OK, just so I know I understand…what about that idea even works for you?

SELLER: Well, as you know, I moved out last month when my new house was built and am having trouble keeping up with the payments on this vacant house.

YOU: So, me guaranteeing you monthly payments will help solve your problem?

SELLER: Yes.

YOU (after a pause for a few seconds): Remember at the beginning of our conversation, I said I only do deals that are good for everyone?

SELLER: Yes.

YOU: How do you see this being a win-win deal?

SELLER: Well, you will help me with my problem of making two payments.

You: And for us?

Seller: You will get a good price on the home and be able to resell it for a profit.

From here, it is just about negotiating the terms and prices. The negotiating strategies I use are beyond what I can talk about here. Do the best you can to get the lowest monthly payments and the longest term. The price should be a lower priority. Also, make sure the seller understands that you are a professional, and you are not in the business to lose money. For that reason, you cannot take over payments on an empty house. You need to have either a few months or make your first payment after you find someone to move in. Do not be afraid of this; the seller will understand.

Sign It Up!

Once you agree to all the terms and you know the seller is comfortable, go to your car and get the agreement. Go quickly over the first two sections, and spend a little time with the provisions. Ask for the seller's help as much as you can, so he or she feels like a participant in the paperwork. You can ask the seller the date, how to spell his or her name and the address, etc.

Sign your name, and give the seller the form to review. Tell him or her to read it and to complete the bottom (try not to say the word "sign" because some sellers will immediately associate signing a form as a negative, even if the agreement is in their best interest). Within 15 seconds of handing the seller the form, start asking questions about the home. Ask about the neighbors, the foundation, what problems he or she has had, etc. Keep asking until the seller signs. This normally helps him or her breeze through the reading and sign quickly. You may also want to see the most recent mortgage statement or get the seller to sign the Authorization to Release Information. Once it is signed, ask if he or she has questions, and then ask how he or she would like to give you access. Either get a key or have the seller commit to putting one in a lockbox.

Go Home and Celebrate

It is important to celebrate success. Take your significant other to dinner or bring home a bottle of champagne. You did a great job and should be rewarded.

I cannot overemphasize the importance of practicing. You will want to practice your routine in the house over and over. Get help role-playing with a spouse, business partner, or friend. Practice in front of the mirror. It is unbelievable how much this will help you when you actually sit down with the seller.

Due Diligence

If you have time the same day, start your due diligence.

put out ads

Title

Call your title company to ask them for an O&E and name search. O&E stands for "owner and encumbrances." You may need to pay for the O&E, but they can also be free. I have just recently started paying five dollars for these. This will tell you who the owner is, the correct spelling, and what liens are on the property.

The name search will let you know if there are any judgments against the owner that could attach to the title. You can also pull the seller's credit report to look for judgments. I know some investors do it that way, but I was always a bit uncomfortable asking the seller if I could pull his or her credit.

Values

You want to know home values and rent values. First, pull comparable sales. If you don't have access to this, call one of your Realtor friends and ask him or her to do it for you. This should also be free because you will be referring business to the Realtor. You can also offer the Realtor a gift or a little money for his or her help. Look at the comps, and be sure that you are looking for what has sold within the last six months. You also want to stay with sold homes close to the subject. I recommend staying within a half mile, if possible. Finally, look for similar houses by looking for houses built around the same time, close to the same size, and with a similar number of bedrooms and bathrooms. Be sure to take things like fireplaces, basements, and garages into consideration. Amenities like garages will have different values in different neighborhoods. You will start to learn what these are worth as you get experience. It is a good idea to drive around the area and look at the comps to get a feel for condition. While you are driving around, look for other homes for sale and for rent. Also ask a lot of questions. Ask Realtors or appraisers you know about amenities and their values in the area.

You can get comparable rentals a couple of ways. First, try the website rentometer.com. Keep in mind that this is not 100 percent accurate, but it will give you an idea. Next, look on the web and in the paper for other homes that are currently for rent. Good places to start are craigslist.org and rentals.com.

Call the owners and ask what amenities the home has, the size, and the rent amount. They will think you are a renter and will be happy to answer your questions. This will give you a good idea what your home will rent for. Finally, you can knock on some doors in the area, tell them you are thinking about renting a home in the neighborhood, and ask if they know what other people are paying for rent. Chances are they will know every house in the area and how much it rents for.

Inspect the Home

If you are concerned about anything with the home, you can hire an inspector or have someone you know go in and look at the property. I generally don't worry about this because I have my seller pay for damages. Also I can get a good feel for how the home has been cared for just by walking through with the owners. If I notice something I want to have checked out, like a foundation issue or an old furnace, I will have my contractor go take a look. There have been times—several, actually—where I ask that the seller put a home warranty in place before I take over.

Understand the Underlying Financing

You need to know what type of financing is in place and how it might impact you. Are there prepayment penalties or is there an adjustable rate note? Is the loan current? You can find this information in one of two ways. You can read the note and get a copy of a recent statement, or you can have the seller sign an authorization for you to get it directly from the loan servicer or lender.

Find the Tenant

You should know within a day if you want to keep the deal or not. If it is not a good enough deal for you, call the seller, and let him or her know. You can always ask for a better deal if you think you can make it work.

Within a day or two, get a lockbox on the home with a key and put out your yard sign. Don't be cheap on the yard signs; have a professional do these for you. Within a week, you should have pictures on the Internet and have signs up in the neighborhood. Handmade signs on poster board may not work well to find sellers, but for some reason they work great to find tenants. Advertise the home as a rent to own with your number. I recommend that when you are getting started and have time, advertise a number you will answer. Your response will be better if you answer your phone.

Price Your Home

Your marketing will start working immediately. In fact, you should expect calls the same day you put out your yard sign. The calls will really increase when you advertise with neighborhood signs and on the Internet, so you will need to have your pricing ready.

I have included a price sheet that I use when I price my homes. This is an idea I received from Peter Conti and David Finkel. My price worksheet looks similar to theirs. I would set the purchase price at or no more than 5 percent higher than the highest comparable sale. You should lock that price in for at least two years. The highest comp must be a legitimate comp; please don't use one that is 4,000 square feet when your home is 750 square feet. Try to find comparable houses that are similar in age, style, size, and amenities. To add 5 percent, you will simply multiply the highest comp by 1.05. For example, if the house is worth $100,000 today, you would multiply $100,000 by 1.05 and get $105,000. Hopefully, you did not agree to pay full price for the home. If you were able to get the home for a price of $90,000, your profit when the tenant buys will be $15,000 in this example.

As for the rent, please refer to the Rent to Own Price Sheet in the appendix for an example. The rent for option 1 will be the market rent. This is what you would rent the home for if it were a normal rental. This number comes from the rent analysis you did from your due diligence. Add $100 to the rent for option 2 and $200 for option 3. You can do anything you want with the rent credits. Remember, rent credits bring down the purchase price, so only be aggressive here if you have enough room in the price with your seller. If there is room, I recommend being very aggressive because chances are the tenant will not buy, and you will be increasing your cash flow. Some investors will set one-year and two-year prices, only offer one payment option, or do a number of other crazy things. Feel free to price it any way you want. Just make sure you are making money.

Field the Calls

As you take calls, get as much information about the prospect as you can. You will want to complete the buyer call sheet as thoroughly as possible. It is important that you find out how much money people have to put down. You don't want to waste your time on people with no money.

If a tenant calls you and does not have money to put down, tell him or her you need at least "X" amount down because you are selling the home on a rent-to-own basis, and you need a commitment from someone who wants to buy. Your conversation will sound like this:

You: And how much money do you have today to put toward owning this home?

TENANT: I have the first month's payment.

You: You know…because we are not renting this house but actually selling this house, we need enough money to let us know you are serious about buying and not renting. We would need at least $5,000. We may be able to work with a little less, but we need some type of financial commitment. What is the most you can come up with?

Explain to the caller this is not a rental and ask the person to please call back if he or she can come up with some more money. Have two or three times a week that you are willing to show the home. Tell all the people who call that they need to come at one of the offered times. Once you know you have people coming, you can tell unqualified people to come also. It will help create competition. The more people you have show up at once, the more stressful for everyone, but the more money you will make and the higher your chances of getting a commitment on the spot. I love this kind of stress because I know it puts cash in my pocket.

My Recent Bidding War

Creating competition works almost every time. Let me explain why it works by giving you an example. This past summer, I was showing a house we were selling on a rent to own. The house did not show all that well, but it was the only rent-to-own home in the area. Because I knew I was the only rent to own, I did not worry about making the house show perfectly.

Competition is great if buyers are competing for your home.

I showed the home to two families. They showed up at the same time and were surprised to see each other. I knew that as soon as they saw someone else looking, they were probably thinking what I did when I looked at the first house I purchased: *Uh-oh...if I don't do something, this other family will get this home.*

Once inside, one family headed upstairs while the other looked around the kitchen. I asked them both to let me know if they had any questions. It was funny; the two families did everything they could to avoid each other. It was almost like the one family was afraid to go upstairs, while the other was afraid to come down. Finally, they switched.

As soon as the family hanging out upstairs came down, the father started to talk to me while the wife and two kids continued their voyage through the house.

The father said, "So, how does this rent-to-own thing work?"

My policy is to talk to all decision makers at once, so I gently said we should wait for his wife. I then started asking him about the house.

"What do you love about the house?" I wanted him to sell himself just like we do with sellers.

He mentioned the master bedroom. He was in no mood to talk, however; he wanted info about the rent to own and fast. He called for his wife to come over. The family upstairs must have caught wind because they hustled down.

"Oh good, everyone is here, so I only need to go through this once," I said. I started by explaining to them that I did not live very close, so I scheduled appointments with more than one family at a time to save on the number of trips I needed to make. They all smiled, looking at each other, and assured me that they understood.

I will call the husband Rick. I use people's names as much as possible because a person's name is that person's favorite word. When we call a person by name, we have a better chance of being liked and trusted.

"OK," I said. "Let's talk about rent to own, but before we do, Rick was just telling me that his favorite part of the house is the master bedroom. What is everyone else's favorite part?" We briefly talked about the house, and before long, I knew I had two families who really wanted my house.

I handed each family a worksheet. I explained it is a very simple concept, but the way I set it up with the payment options can get confusing, so I like to write it down to help me explain it. They both seemed to appreciate that. I then went over the worksheet. We started with the price. I typically spend less than 10 seconds on this unless I get an objection. I then explained what a rent credit is. I went through the options, explaining that the only thing that changes is the rental amount and the amount of rent credit they get. I finished with the option consideration and explained that it is nonrefundable and applied toward the purchase. What happened next was common and is still amusing. I found myself hosting a bidding war.

"I have the full $5,000, and I can go home and get it right now," one gentleman said.

The other said, "I can have the $5,000 by Friday, but I will pay you $1,000 right now to hold it for me, and I will give you an extra $50 a month."

The other guy responded, "I can do that, too."

I let this go on for a little while, as I was trying not to explode with joy, knowing this was a done deal.

This may not be the best advice, because most of the time, if someone wants to give you money, you take it. I told them both to complete the application, and they both made comments that they wanted to talk to me about their situations. This is common if they have bad credit, or they are not looking at a rent to own. I assured them I would talk to them each separately, but I needed the application, and if they would each give me one month's payment, I would hold the home and make sure one of them got it. I explained I had another appointment scheduled in a few days. I did have another appointment scheduled in my calendar, but I hadn't filled the slot. Simply stating that there was another appointment made them want to give me the deposit. After all, if they gave me the deposit, they had a fifty-fifty chance of getting it.

I took the deposits and the applications and went home to screen the prospects. I picked the best one and moved the family in. I took away their option of going home and thinking about it before they made their deposits, which is one of the biggest objections you will get. By creating competition, I also eliminated the option to negotiate with me on my price or terms. In fact, the opposite came true. I was able to get more than my original price and terms.

Get a Deposit

The objective of every showing or appointment is to get the prospect to commit by giving you a deposit. Again, you can see the Deposit Receipt I use in the appendix. It is a nonrefundable deposit, so if you are holding the home for the prospect and he or she backs out, you will keep the deposit. This is why I always try to get one month's payment. I am willing, however, to get anything just so the prospect feels committed. If the deposit is too small to make me feel that he or she is truly committed, I continue marketing and showing the home but will not rent it to someone else unless the first prospect is denied or changes his or her mind.

Always, always, always ask for the deposit.

Finish the Paperwork

Now that you have a deposit and feel good about the deal, you can go ahead and finish signing everything with your seller. Up to this point, you were able to walk away from the deal because of the wording in your contract. Now that you know you want to move forward, you need all the correct paperwork in place so that you are protected. When you first met with the seller and went over the contract, you explained that you would need to get him or her to sign some additional paperwork.

Schedule a time you can meet with the seller in front of a notary. There are several travel notary services out there if you want to meet the seller in his or her home. You can also meet at a bank like Steph and I did on our first deal. Get all the other paperwork signed, and be sure to have the Option Affidavit and the deed of trust or mortgage notarized and recorded. You can use your O&E to get the correct legal address. Do not make mistakes on these two forms. It is very important that you have the seller's name and the property's legal address exactly as it appears on the title.

Finally, you will call the insurance agent to get a fax number or e-mail address. Let the agent know you are sending a letter from the owner asking that you be added to the policy. At this second meeting with the seller, I will ask for a copy of the note for his or her mortgage if I have not already collected this. You might choose to pay the seller directly and expect him or her to make the payment to the lender. If that is the case, you will need to keep tabs on the loan to protect your investment. You can do this with the authorization. What I like to do is get the seller's account login info so I can get online and check the account.

All this paperwork may seem confusing, but it really isn't. Just read through each form a few times so you have a good understanding of what it says.

Sign the Lease

Your tenant buyer is now ready to move in. It is time to meet to sign the lease, sign the option, and collect your money. I hear the sound of cash registers in my head while I am driving to these appointments. I really love these appointments for more than the money, though. These families love me; they are getting a chance to own a home, and they are normally very excited. Oftentimes I get hugs, and sometimes I get gifts. One lady ran a gift-basket business and gave Steph and me a basket full of cool coffee mugs, hot chocolate, cookies, and a bunch of other goodies we probably did not need. But it was awesome!

This is normally a pretty fast appointment, but there will be a few questions. You may hear other people tell you to meet somewhere other than the property. The idea is that you do not want the tenant buyer looking around for things that are wrong with the place while you are signing the lease. I don't know that it really makes a difference; I normally just meet him or her at the house. Get there early enough to remove anything that belongs to you. Sometimes I use fake plants and pictures to help bring the property to life while it is vacant.

Finally, when you go over the lease, be sure to spend a few extra minutes on the part about the tenant buyer's payments. Of course the tenant will say he or she will never pay late, but you need to be sure the tenant understands what happens if he or she does, and be sure he or she understands that this is a business to you and that you take late payments seriously. I go into detail about the eviction process and how expensive my late fee is. My policy is to charge 6 percent of the payment amount in late fees if the payment is not made by the third of the month. If I don't get payment by the fifth, I post the eviction notice. I also explain that if the tenant plans to pay by mail, the postmark means nothing to me. It must be in my box on time, and I do not care if it is lost in the mail. Sound harsh? You must say this, or every late payment will be the fault of the post office. I suggest setting up Auto Pay as much as possible. You can do this with your bank or use the website secure.depositexpress.com.

Something I have not tried but have heard works well is setting up a savings account at your bank and giving your tenant deposit slips. Have the tenant make the deposit directly into your account. You will want it to be a savings account so he or she cannot withdraw money with a forged check, and you will want to transfer the money out of the account quickly to keep it at a low balance. I am going to say this again: do not meet your tenant or allow your tenant to bring you rent. Your time is too valuable, and you do not want to give control to your tenant. Remember, you are in charge, and the tenant must play by your rules. A little thing like this will really help keep any tenant from trying to take advantage of you later.

I also spend a little time reviewing the liability section of the lease and strongly encourage the tenant to get his or her own renters' insurance policy. If there is a fire or flood, my insurance does not cover the tenant's belongings. I do not require renters' insurance, but many investors do. It is something you should consider requiring your tenant to carry.

REHAB BRIDGE LOANS

Most home-buying strategies are referred to by the type of financing used. For example, we just talked about buying homes using a lease option. It does not matter how you found the home; if you used a lease with an option to acquire it, it will be referred to as a lease option. The same is true with a traditional transaction. It does not matter how you found the home; if you use a mortgage with nothing else, I would consider that traditional. Now, if you take a traditional financing method and couple that with a rehab bridge loan, you have something really special. What this will create for you is little-to-no-money-down acquisitions where you will have instant cash-flowing properties with instant equity. There is a little more risk with this strategy because you will be signing on loans, and there are some limitations, so you might want to start with the lease-option strategy first, and once you master that, add this to your arsenal.

If you are uncomfortable calling or meeting with sellers or any other aspect of the lease-option strategy, this is a great alternative that is much more conventional.

The basic idea of this deal is to find a property in disrepair that you can rehab and add value to. You can buy these with short-term private money or hard money and get 100 percent financing to buy and fix it. Once the property is repaired, you would refinance the loan into a traditional loan. There are several keys to making this work.

Adding Value

A typical hard-money lender will loan you 65 percent to 70 percent of the after-repaired value (ARV). My company, Pine Financial Group Inc., loans 70 percent of the ARV. When you are working on your refinance, the appraiser will need to justify a large increase in value from what you paid for the house.

Let's take a $100,000 home as an example to keep this simple. If the house is worth $100,000, once it is repaired, you can get a loan for $70,000 (if you use a hard-money lender who will loan 70 percent). If it needs $15,000 in improvements or repairs to hit the $100,000 value, you can pay up to about $50,000 for that house and have no money out of pocket. $50,000 purchase + $15,000 repairs = $65,000, leaving you $5,000 to cover closing costs. As soon as that property is ready, you can refinance at 75 percent loan to value (LTV), which is the current LTV guideline for Fannie Mae, and roll in all the closing costs to refinance. We will look at more examples later, but you can see that for this to work, you need to get a great deal, add a lot of value through repairs, or better yet, have a combination of both. In this example, we show an increase in value of $50,000, which sounds like a lot but is really not that hard to justify with some great repairs.

No Title Seasoning

Now that you are falling in love with this strategy, I am guessing you want to start calling lenders to see if this is really true. Some mortgage brokers or bankers will tell you that you can't do this. They will say that you need to be on title for six or twelve months before you can refinance if you want to use the appraised value. This is simply not true. Fannie Mae has no title-seasoning requirement, meaning they can refinance you the day after you buy a house and use an appraised value, not your purchase price, as the value in the underwriting process. The problem with most mortgage professionals is they are not selling directly to Fannie Mae, and even when they are, their company is still tightening up the rules. So when they say they can't do it, they are telling the truth. "They" probably can't.

The tightening of the rules I am talking about is called a "lender overlay." Most lenders these days are selling their loans to Fannie Mae, and it is extremely important to them that Fannie Mae buys these loans. For that reason, they take Fannie Mae guidelines and add some of their own to make extra sure Fannie Mae will buy the loan. Each rule that is in addition to Fannie Mae guidelines is called an overlay. Title seasoning, or the amount of time you must own the house, is an extremely common overlay. So if you get the response that you need to season the title or own the house longer, understand that it is just an overlay and that you need to call someone else.

If Fannie Mae ever changes its guidelines, it could affect this strategy, but the worst case would be you needing to carry the high-cost bridge loan until you meet any title-seasoning requirements. Any changes to current Fannie Mae guidelines should not prevent you from using this strategy.

Location of the Property

You can probably use this strategy anywhere, but it works best in areas of town that have a good rent-to-price ratio. I am not going to give you specific numbers to look for, but I will say it is much harder to use this strategy with higher price point houses. The discount you need is greater, the value you need to add is larger, and it is harder to get them to cash flow. Start by looking at areas near you with lower-priced homes.

Risks and Limitations

Appraisal

This is the largest risk you will face with this strategy, so it is important to understand this going in. In a perfect world, the appraisal for your refinance will come in at the same value as the appraisal when you purchase the property. The reality is that an appraisal is just someone's opinion of value, and opinions can vary. If the appraisal on the refinance comes in lower than you want or expected, you might need to either switch to a new lender and get a new appraisal (for another fee, of course) or bring money to closing to cover the difference in values. This is important to know, because although you can buy properties with little or no money down, it does not mean you should not have some money set aside in reserve.

Limited on Number of Deals You Can Do

Because this strategy works best with Fannie Mae loans, you will want to consider the Fannie Mae property-limit guidelines. As I write this section, Fannie Mae will allow a borrower to own up to 10 financed properties, including your primary home. This limit is for investment-property purchases and refinances only, so actually, you can have a total of 11 financed properties if your 11th property is your primary. The guidelines get stricter after you have four financed properties, so be sure to check with your preferred lender to understand if you are going to qualify. If you are doing business in a market that Pine Financial Group, Inc. services, you can get lender and other referrals on our "Pine Recommends" page on our website, PineFinancialGroup.com.

Personally Liable

Because you will own the house and be signing on the debt, you are personally going to be liable for it. This is not a big deal if you are buying good properties, but it is something to be aware of. This, of course, is much different from the lease options we discussed earlier.

There Is No Help from a Seller for Repairs

Because you own the house, there is no seller you can call to cover major repairs. The help from the seller is a huge advantage to the lease option. To mitigate this risk, you can use a home warranty, but once you have several properties, it is probably better to just keep a reserve and handle repairs yourself.

Want more information on this strategy? Check out the *free* special report or video on our website, PineFinancialGroup.com.

Generate Leads (Lots of Them)

Just like buying a home with a lease option, you need a lot of homes to look at for this strategy to work. For this strategy, you are looking for houses needing work that you can add value to. Once again, this is very different than a lease option, which I consider the "pretty-home business" because it works best for homes that don't need work.

The three ways I suggest finding this type of property, whether you plan to move into it or rent it, are through Realtors, wholesalers, and direct mail.

Realtors

Realtors are great. You can really rely on them when you are getting started. They can do all the research as far as valuation, how long homes have been for sale, and what kinds of seller concessions are common in the area. They will do the work of scanning the multiple listing service (MLS) and may even drive you around to look at properties. Typically, you do not pay for Realtor services directly because it is the responsibility of the seller to be sure everyone gets paid. This is the strategy I think most of you will pursue because it is the easiest and most common. I would not rely solely on a Realtor, but it is good to use one as much as possible, assuming he or she can find you deals, of course.

When you look for a Realtor, my suggestion would be to ask people you know for referrals. Call several Realtors, and ask them questions about their experience. You want to know how long they have been a Realtor, how often they have changed companies, what their typical client looks like, how many rentals they personally have, and who manages them. You will obviously want to pick the Realtor who has the most investor clients, has his or her own investments, and appears to have adequate experience. You will also want to have a personal connection with the Realtor. This will be a very valuable relationship for you in your business, so take your time and pick the best. With that said, you will likely work with several until you find the right one for you. I like Realtors who are in their first few years and don't have a list of clients. I want to be a friend to them and be their biggest buyer, so they call me first.

I also want to mention that although the Realtor will do a lot for you for free, please don't take advantage of that. As often as you can, close on houses so they get paid, and send them referrals when you meet with sellers you are unable to help.

I would also stay away from signing an exclusive agreement with a Realtor that would prevent you from working with another agent who brought you a deal. Most will ask you to sign an agreement, but it is not necessary. I recommend asking them to prove they can find you quality deals before you commit and that you are happy to sign an agreement for an individual deal if that is what they need. I like working with multiple Realtors because I like multiple sources for deals.

Wholesalers

These people are fantastic, and I absolutely love working with them. If you have a few good wholesalers on your team, they alone can keep your real estate funnel full.

> **Wholesalers are great to use if you don't have time to look at a lot of potential deals.**

A wholesaler is someone who has the skill of finding great deals. He or she simply takes control of a home—normally by putting it under contract—and then sells his or her interest in the home to an investor. The wholesaler will take a small fee for this service. Here is an example of a typical deal from a wholesaler:

The wholesaler gets a home under contract for $50,000. The home needs $15,000 worth of repairs. After the home is fixed up, it will be worth $100,000. The wholesaler sells the house for $55,000.

In this example, an investor like you or me will be buying a house for $55,000 and putting $15,000 into it. We will own a repaired home for $70,000 that is worth $100,000. This obviously does not take into account fees and costs associated with the transaction, but my point is that you can get some great deals, and you don't even need to find them.

There are a few common ways wholesalers will sell you a home. They may double close, assign the contract, or assign the interest in an entity.

Double Close

They can buy the house and sell you the house back-to-back. The way this typically works is your money will be wired to the title company or attorney. With the money there, the title company will allow the wholesaler to close with the original seller, putting him or her on title. Literally minutes after this closing, you will buy the house from the wholesaler. Once all the documents are signed, the wholesaler will fund the two deals with the money sitting in escrow. In some cases, the title company or even the state will require funds for both transactions, in which case the wholesaler would need a loan for a day or would need to wire in the money for the day. Once everything is closed, the title company will record the deed from the original owner to the wholesaler first and then immediately record the deed from the wholesaler to you. The wholesaler is on title for a few seconds or however long it actually takes the county to record two deeds.

You must have your own cash or line of credit, or you will need to work with a hard-money or private lender who understands this type of closing. Lenders generally hate this because they are sending money to close on a house that the seller has not taken title to.

Title companies are becoming less comfortable with these, but my company, Pine Financial Group, Inc., is still funding these for our clients.

Assign the Contract

Assigning the contract is much, much easier. The fee can be disclosed on the settlement statement, just like a Realtor's commission, and you will close with the original seller. In this case, the wholesaler is giving you the rights to the contract for a fee. You will sign an assignment and take a copy of the original contract so you can read what you are agreeing to. Once the assignment is executed, you will send it to the title company and close in the place of the original buyer. Although I still see a few of these a month, this, too, is becoming much more challenging. In fact, most banks or lenders selling their foreclosures (REOs and HUDs) will not accept assignable contracts. They will specifically remove the assignability out of the agreement. Their position is that they want the best price for the house they can get, and they do not want to see it resold for a profit. But investors are creative and have learned how to get around this.

Assign Interest in an Entity

This is 100 percent legal, and we see this multiple times a month. The way this works is the wholesaler will set up what I like to call a "throw away" entity, meaning it has one purpose, and then it is worthless. These entities are normally LLCs, but we are also seeing trusts. Once the entity is established, the wholesaler will make offers in that entity name as the buyer. When he or she gets a deal under contract, he or she sells the entity to the investor. Once the new investor is the owner of the entity, the investor closes on the house, signing as owner of the entity that has the contract. Once closed, you can transfer title to another entity of your choice. This is a pretty advanced topic, so once again, you need to work with lenders who really understand the ins and outs of wholesaling.

Wholesalers sell these properties at discounts for several reasons. Most often they just do not want the hassle of fixing and owning the house. It is a great deal for them because they never use their own cash or credit, have no risk, and will make a fee on a house they never own. Sometimes these wholesalers find more houses than they can handle, so instead of turning down a good deal, they are happy making a little by passing it on.

I have wholesaled deals myself for a quick profit. I did it because the houses needed more work than I wanted to do or were in areas I did not like.

You can find these wholesalers by talking to other investors. Go to places other investors hang out, like real estate investment groups, and ask around. You will want to get on as many wholesale buyer lists as you can. Once you show you can and will perform, wholesalers will start calling you about new deals before they even send them out to their buyer list.

A final word of caution: some—but not all—wholesalers are less than ethical. It is your responsibility to perform your own due diligence and not to believe a word any wholesaler says.

Direct Mail

I personally think you will find your best deals with direct mail. It is going to take time and a financial commitment, so it is not for everyone. The biggest key to direct mail being successful is consistency. Each person should get five to eight pieces of mail from you. I also think you need to send out 500 or more a week to see any real results. This strategy is how many of the wholesalers I know find their deals.

A few ideas for mailing lists include probates, vacant properties, stale or expired listings, out-of-town owners, evictions, FSBOs, free-and-clear properties, and bankruptcies. You can get these lists from county records searches (actually going to the county buildings is the best), Realtors, driving through neighborhoods, or list brokers. There are a lot more lists you can mail to, but these are the lists that I have mailed to and actually bought houses from. I like to mix in postcards and letters. Postcards are great because they do not need to be opened and are cheap to send, but letters play a very important role in your campaign. In fact, I think you will find that better results come from the letters than the postcards.

Analyze Deals and Make Offers

Now that you have a large number of leads and you are looking at a lot of homes, it is time to actually take action and buy something. I want to briefly discuss analyzing deals and how to make your offers. You will obviously want to make sure you can come up with the money to follow through on your contract, so go make contact with a private or hard-money lender and also get approved for that refinance.

As mentioned before, when you are getting started, you will want to connect with a Realtor to help you. The Realtor should have experience and should give you his or her opinion on many things, but most important is the value of the home once it is repaired.

Let's keep this simple. Make sure the home will rent for more than the amount your payment will be once the refinance is done. Have your mortgage broker help you come up with a payment amount, or you can use an amortization calculator found online. Simply Google "amortization calculator," and you will have several great ones to choose from. You can also get free apps for your smart phone. You do not want to buy based on thoughts or feelings of future appreciation, at least not on your first few deals. Yes, you will get appreciation over time, but your first priority has to be to protect your monthly cash flow. *Do not* get into a situation where you need to feed your properties every month. They either take care of themselves financially, or you don't buy them, period!

After you determine at what offer your property will cash flow, you want to look at the lending requirements and use that to help steer your offer. For example, my company loans 70 percent of the after-repaired value, so if you want to keep your down payment under $5,000, you will want to figure the after-repaired value and multiply that by 0.70 to figure out how much money you will be able to borrow. Use the maximum loan as a guide to help you come up with your offer.

Once you have the house under contract, you should really dig into your diligence. It does not make a lot of sense to spend too much time until you have it under contract. In the beginning, you may want to have the home inspected. I do not hire inspectors because they are so concerned with protecting themselves that they don't always give me the best advice. This is just my experience. I am sure there are plenty of good home in-spectors out there; I just don't use them. Most things you can see yourself. For the things you can't see, have an expert in that area come take a look. For example, if you are worried about the foundation, pay an engineer to come. You may want to have an HVAC person come look at the heating and air conditioning. It is a good idea to have the sewer line examined. If the home is older, or you just think you need it, have a plumber or electri-cian come. I know this seems like a lot of work and may be a little more expensive than a home inspector, but I believe it is worth knowing what you are buying. Ask other investors for referrals for all these professionals.

You will also need to put together a scope of work or a repair budget for the hard-money lender, so you might want contractors to come out and give you bids. Plan on getting your bids and budget done quickly. Most contracts will give you a certain amount of time to get all your inspec-tions done and allow you out of the contract without a penalty if you find something you are not comfortable with. If that inspection deadline passes, your earnest money might be at risk, so move quickly.

Making the Offer

If you are buying the home from a wholesaler, you will probably want to do your due diligence before you enter into an agreement. There are two reasons for this:

1. Oftentimes you are entering into an agreement you can't get out of without losing your earnest money.
2. You do not want to back out of deals with wholesalers because they are valuable to you, and you do not want them thinking you will back out of other deals. If a wholesaler thinks there is the potential of you backing out, he or she will stop providing you with deals. You want to be known as someone who closes so deals keep presenting themselves. The investor community is smaller than you might think, and you do not want a bad reputation.

A simple formula to make an offer is based on the maximum loan amount. You start with the end value and multiply it by the percent your hard-money or private lender will lend. Again, we lend 70 percent, so you will multiply the value by 0.70 to come up with the maximum loan. If you have $5,000 that you are willing to put down, add that to the maximum loan amount. From that number, subtract the closing costs you will need to buy the house, and subtract the money it will take to complete your repairs. You will want to ask the hard-money lender for a little help coming up with the closing costs. We charge 4 percent origination, and there are other fees that need to be accounted for, so we tell our clients to count on 4 percent of the loan amount, plus about $2,000. Let's look at an example so you can see how to make this offer.

In this example, let's assume you have $5,000 to get this deal closed. You think the house will be worth $140,000, and it needs approximately $20,000 in repairs.

First, calculate the maximum you can borrow:

$$\$140,000 \text{ (value) x } 70\% = \$98,000 \text{ (max loan)}$$

Then add the $5,000 that you are willing to use:

$$\$98,000 + \$5,000 = \$103,000$$

Then calculate the closing costs:

$$\$98,000 \text{ (loan) x } 4\% + \$2,000 = \$5,920$$

Finally, subtract the closing costs and the repair budget:

$$\$103,000 - \$5,920 - \$20,000 = \$77,080$$

Your offer on this house should be $77,080 or less.

If you are interested in some free worksheets to help you with your offers (they work great for fix and flips), you can get them on our website, PineFinancialGroup.com, under "Resources."

If you are buying from an owner or through a Realtor, be sure you have a clause in your contract that allows you to inspect the property before you commit, like we talked about above. This is referred to as an "inspection clause" or "inspection contingency." The beauty here is that you can make offers on homes, get them under contract, *and* get your earnest money back if you find something that you don't like. Getting a property under contract commits the seller to sell while giving you time to decide whether or not to buy. This allows you to make offers without even looking at the house and allows you to make a lot of offers in the shortest amount of time. Again, for the sake of your reputation with Realtors, do not make offers on houses you don't intend to buy. Make the offers low, and only back out if your diligence suggests it.

The inspection clause is probably built into the agreement you would use with a Realtor. If you are using your own contract, it could be something as simple as this:

Inspection Clause: This agreement is subject to a final inspection and written approval of the property by the buyer. (You can add a date or deadline if you like.)

Due Diligence

Again, if you are buying from a wholesaler, do this prior to entering into an agreement; otherwise, start this immediately after signing a contract with a seller. Due diligence will be almost the same when buying a home traditionally as it is when you buy using a lease option. There are two important differences:

1. Spend plenty of time making sure you know every lien that can be attached to the property when buying on a lease option. You will probably not be buying title insurance, so it is your responsibility to know who owns the home and all encumbrances. When you buy traditionally, you and the seller will be buying title insurance, so you would be more certain you are getting clear title.
2. Spend time inspecting the home for things you can't see when buying traditionally. Once you close on the house, the seller has no more obligations, so if you miss something while inspecting the home, it will be your responsibility to fix it. Although I don't use

inspectors, this is why you might consider hiring one. Oftentimes, when you buy on a lease option, you will negotiate with the seller to take care of major problems, so an inspection is less important. Notice I said *less* important and did not say *not* important. It is still important to view the home and look for obvious problems.

If the seller on a lease option is selling because the person has no money, don't expect a lot of help from the seller if something goes wrong. In this case, you may want to spend a little extra time with your inspection.

Find the Tenant
This step is going to be the same no matter how you buy the home. Please refer to our earlier discussion on finding tenants.

TURN YOUR INVESTING INTO A BUSINESS

There cannot be more truth than a statement I learned early on. I don't even remember where I first heard it, but I have heard it over and over. The statement is simple:

Treat your investing as a business.

Real estate investing is a business and must be treated as such. Yes, it is fun, but it is not a hobby. Some people collect coins and stamps; I collect houses and have a blast doing it, but I take it seriously.

Sellers and tenants are clients. You cannot blow them off, and you need to follow up. The bottom line is you need guidelines and systems in place just like any successful business.

Get a Mentor

I learned early on to find mentors and grab hold of their coattails. Let the mentor drag you around for a while.

After our first two creative deals, which took us nearly a year to complete, we decided to spend a little money and learn better ways of doing business. We joined a mentorship program. Who better to work with than Peter Conti and David Finkel? After all, it was because of their book we had two deals in the first place.

We committed to their program, which was not cheap, especially since we were eating a lot of rice and Top Ramen at that time. We spread out the enrollment fees over several credit cards and within weeks received the home-study course in the mail. We dug right in.

I can't remember how long it was, but I would say within a month of studying their material, we went to a three-day boot camp that walked us through lease-option investing. We actually made calls to potential sellers and went to an appointment at the event. There was a ton of role-playing and hands-on practice.

The Monday after the training, we hit the ground running. We used the excitement and motivation from the weekend as momentum and started making calls to sellers immediately. We made calls on breaks between college classes and lunch breaks at work. We scheduled as many appointments as possible. We did not necessarily want to get deals right away (although that would have been nice) but wanted to get good at being in the seller's house. We wanted our practice so when we started paying for marketing, we would have the skills to convert leads to deals.

I want to say a few things about national mentorships. Most national mentors don't really know what they are doing; they don't do deals themselves and are too large to actually give you the support you need. Most national gurus will overcharge and under deliver. For example, we paid $5,500, but I have heard some mentorships cost as much as $40,000. David and Peter are no longer working together, but they were the exception as mentors. Be very careful with your search for a mentor, and when in doubt, stay local.

Mastermind Group

We also joined a mastermind group. This group consisted of three other investors who were not out there kicking tires. Everyone in this group was buying houses. We met on the phone once a week to talk about our businesses and to help each other through the challenges. This was also used for accountability. We each would make promises to the group about what we would accomplish before the next call. I strongly encourage you to join or form a group like this. Each person in the group must have the same goal of helping everyone get better. You will want to hold each other accountable and share knowledge and motivation. We all know that starting a business is not easy, and there will be ups and downs. You can lean on this group during the hard times.

Take a minute and write down names of at least ten people you know who are like-minded and from whom you can benefit. Call these people and ask them if they are willing to be in a small group that meets twice or more a month. Don't just call your friends; call people who intimidate you. These may be people who don't know you, but you know they have had success. This is about getting out of your comfort zone and improving your life. They very well may say no, but who knows? They may say, "Yes!"

From what I have read, the first person to form a group like this was Benjamin Franklin. Franklin used mastermind groups to help him and his colleagues amass fortunes. You can do the same. You will learn more about mastermind groups by reading *Think and Grow Rich* by Napoleon Hill (Hill 1937). This is a must-read for all business owners.

Although we no longer have our mastermind call with our original group, we are all still close friends. When I was starting Pine Financial, I used this same strategy with a different group that included a very successful investor, Realtor, attorney, and title-company owner. I've had successful results each time I participated in a group like this.

Marketing Business

One of the most successful people in business I know claims that no matter what service or product we are selling, we are all in the marketing business. No matter what business you are in or whom you work for, nobody can get paid if there isn't someone making a sale. To take it a step further, nobody can make a sale without a prospect. And where do prospects come from? Marketing.

Marketing does not just mean mailing postcards or running classified ads. Marketing is happening every time you talk to someone, hand out a card, or when anyone else talks about you or hands out your card. Marketing occurs whenever you answer your friend's questions about how business is going or answer your phone.

There are several great books on this subject, and I highly recommend books by Dan Kennedy. You can look him up or search for his books on the Internet. The basic concept for a real estate business is to stay consistent, but you must first select your medium. How do you want to attract your sellers and your tenants? As I said before, my suggestion for buying homes with a lease option is to focus on using the phone and bandit signs. These are cheap, and they work. Some other things that have worked really well include:

- Direct mail to probate houses (these lists can be compiled from newspapers or public records or purchased from list brokers)
- Direct mail to FSBOs and FRBOs (create this list from the classifieds using reverse lookup at anywho.com)
- Direct mail to expired and stale listings (obtained from a Realtor; these are houses that have been listed with a Realtor but have not sold)
- Knocking on doors (foreclosures, FSBOs, or in areas you want to buy)
- Networking

Things we have done that were not as successful but have heard worked well for others:

- Radio ads
- Door flyers
- Grocery-store flyers
- Mailing to foreclosures
- Calling foreclosures
- Mailing to zip codes
- Mass faxes (you can actually get in trouble for this one)
- Newspaper ads

Once you pick the medium, start doing it. Do it every week, and do the same amount. For example, we hung 20 signs per week and made 20 calls per day.

Use scripts. Whenever you talk to someone, you want to say the same things over and over. When you get those calls during dinner, doesn't it sound like the caller has a script? Why is that? *Because it works!*

Have a follow-up system. We talked about this earlier, but it is worth repeating. I can't tell you how many deals we got just because we were the only investors who would follow up. I told you about our system with the accordion file, but there may be better ways. For Pine Financial I now use ACT, but I know a lot of people who use Outlook. ACT is great because it allows me to keep notes on everyone and set follow-up dates. Each day I pull up ACT, it gives me a list of people to follow up with that day.

Finally, the most important piece to marketing is knowing what your results are. Keep track of everything: how many calls it takes you to set an appointment, how many appointments to get a deal, etc.

Once you start spending money, know how much it takes to get your phone to ring with one lead for each medium. I averaged close to $50 per call I received, and it took me 20 calls to get one deal. So for every

$1,000 I spent, I bought a house. Bandit signs were closer to $25 per call, and direct mail was closer to $40. Flyers, radio ads, and other things I was testing cost more per call. With this information, you will know what you need to do to get deals and where to spend your money.

I kept track by making a tick mark under a *C* every time I made contact. If that contact turned into an appointment, I made a tick mark under an *A*. If I signed that deal up, I made a mark under a *D*. Finally, if I put a tenant in the home and kept the deal, I made a tick mark under an *S* for success! I made these marks on a dry-erase whiteboard, and each week I would move them into an Excel spreadsheet. I kept track per month. After I was good meeting and negotiating with sellers, I tried to limit my appointments. A typical month would look something like this:

C	A	D	S
20	3	1	1

This would be 20 calls for three appointments, one deal, and one success. Success means I decide to keep the deal after I do all my due diligence. I learned this system from Peter Conti and David Finkel in their mentorship program.

Once you graduate from signs and calling for cash, you will definitely want to use direct mail. Direct mail is my favorite marketing medium because you can pinpoint your target market. Also, you can qualify your leads with your marketing. This means you can write in the letter or postcard exactly what you are looking for and weed out people who may call with something you are *not* looking for. For example, if you want to put together lease options, you want nicer homes in nicer areas. You can put in your letter that you want homes that need little to no work and are willing to pay full price for them. If you want a house you can fix up, you may want to put in your letter that you buy houses in any condition. This will make your call quality higher, and you can spend less time with unqualified leads.

Direct mail is more about the list than the message. The message is important, and you will want to tweak and test it and keep coming up with something that works a little better, but your focus needs to start with obtaining a good list. The easiest and most effective list I have ever used to do lease options is stale listings. (Probate lists have worked the best for fix and flips.) Stale listings are Realtor listings that are about to expire. Other Realtors cannot market to this list because it is a violation of a rule they have. As soon as the listing expires, it is fair game, and the homeowner will get nailed with letters and postcards from Realtors and investors. With a stale listing, chances are very high that your letters are the only ones the homeowner is getting and that you will catch the owner before he or she extends the listing with the Realtor.

To get this list, call your Realtor friend and tell him or her what you want. Narrow it down by two zip codes, beds, baths, and price. I would give my Realtor two zip codes and tell him I want all listings that will expire in the next 45 days that are at least three bedrooms, two bathrooms, and are priced between $150,000 and $250,000. I normally get back a list of several hundred. If the list is more or less than you want, adjust your criteria. Once you have this list, look through it and reduce it to the number of pieces you want to send. I always did 200. Now you can look up each house and get the owner's name and mailing address, or you can mail directly to the property if you don't have time. You can also hire someone to do it, but I suggest getting the owner's information so you can use it on the envelope or label. It is more likely to be opened if a name is on it. You will also get correct addresses in case the owner does not live in the home. If you have no time, you can simply mail to the property, and most will get forwarded to the owner.

One final thought on direct mail. You need to send at least five pieces to every address, and you should send consistently. Some people will suggest two or more a week. I suggest sending one piece per week for five or more weeks. I start with a small postcard and do not expect too many calls.

Postcards are cheaper to send, and you will get updated addresses and returned mail for failure to locate the owner. Once you get these back, update your list. I then send four letters, each one referring to the postcard or the letter before it. For example, I will say something like, "Hi, it's me again. Did you get the letter I sent you last week? I was just following up to tell you…"

You can do things like offer a free report to help increase your success. Don't expect too many calls. You should have a success rate with this mailing of around 5 percent. So with your list of 200, you will get about 10 calls that month, and they will probably come on the third and fourth mailing. Other mailing lists will probably have a lower success rate. Remember, marketing is a numbers game.

Keep Good Records

All successful businesses keep records and have systems in place for record keeping. You should be no different. Here are my suggestions to consider:

- **Separate bank account.** Chances are high that you have or will set up an entity other than yourself. I suggest an LLC when you are getting started, because they are much easier to understand than corporations or different types of partnerships and provide similar protection. You will want to set up a bank account in the name of your company and for obvious reasons keep good records when money comes into or leaves the account.

Name your business something that does not reference investing or home buying. Lenders hate investors because statistically, investors carry additional risk. Some underwriters will not lend to you if they know your company's primary function is investing. If you plan to go full time, I suggest a business name that does not suggest what you do. I know this contradicts conventional wisdom, but trust me on this.

When you are ready to set up your account, shop around. There are several banks that allow small-business checking for free. I have a free account with an unlimited number of transactions.

- **Books.** You will want to set up company books as soon as you get a property.

QuickBooks is the absolute best program for bookkeeping, and all CPAs I have ever talked to like to see their clients using QuickBooks. My advice is to be very aggressive with your tax deductions, but do it legally and keep great records.

For help with setting up and maintaining your business books, I recommend John Hyre's home-study course *The Real Estate Investor's KISS Guide to Bookkeeping* (Hyre 2002). This course will walk you step-by-step through setting up and maintaining books. The course also comes with a CD that has a template of a real estate investment company with all the accounts already set up. It is not simple to add a property to your books, and if you do it wrong, you will lose out on potential tax deductions.

- **Database.** In reference to sellers, we briefly talked about how you want to have some type of system for following up. It would benefit you to keep the names and contact info for everyone you will potentially do business with, as well as any professionals in the industry. When I say professional, I am referring to appraisers, attorneys, Realtors, mortgage brokers, maintenance people, accountants, other investors, and so on. A database is one of the most valuable assets to the business. It is critical to have the ability to send out a mass e-mail or mailings. Start building a database the day you go into business, and constantly update and add to it using a software system like Outlook or ACT.
- **Maintenance.** This has never happened to me, but I have heard horror stories about other investors getting into some trouble for

not maintaining a rental. It has caused problems, like not being able to collect rent that was due, among other things. The scary thing is the tenants may not always tell you when there is a problem but may tell a judge they did. This is especially common if they are behind on rent.

For any maintenance request over $50, I demand that my tenant call me with the request *and* send it to me in writing. I keep all these requests in my files. If a problem ever arises, I can provide documentation that the request must be in writing (it says this in my lease) and that I keep files for all maintenance requests. I don't know for sure, but my thought is if I keep records for all requests and state that I did not receive one from the tenant, it will look favorable to a judge. It is also easy to have maintenance issues slip your mind, especially when you are managing multiple units, so if it is in writing, you will have a reminder to make sure it is resolved. I tack the request to a board and do not file it until the issue is resolved. Remember, tenants are your clients and pay your bills, so take care of them.

- **Files.** Create a file system that will allow you to retrieve documents with very little effort. It is essential that you can find leases, contracts, invoices, or anything else when you need them. I recommend buying a filing cabinet that is separate from any personal files and have a separate file for each property. My system is to have a hanging file for each property, and we have a manila folder inside the hanging file for documents related to the seller (if the deal is a lease option or subject to), a separate folder for documents related to the tenant (leases, applications, etc.), and one for expenses. We have separate files for bank statements and other documents not related to a specific property like phone bills, CPA letters, and business invoices. Keep past tenant information for several years. We keep all prior tenant files for four years.
- **Journal.** This is arguably the most critical file you may have in the early stages of business. I strongly believe you should keep

a journal and write in it often. This will help you accelerate your growth.

This does not have to be hard. My journal was a spiral notebook I left in the car. Anytime Steph or I went on an appointment with a seller, we wrote in the journal. As soon as we left, we would pull around the corner, stop the car, and write down these three things:

- A summary of the appointment
- Things we did well
- Things we could improve

You may want to expand and keep a journal for how the entire day went, but at the very least, keep one for houses you look at and sellers you meet.

Celebrate Your Success

This probably does not sound all that important; at least that is what I thought. But it is! It feels good to reach your goals, but it actually feels better, and goals are easier to obtain, if there is a reward. I suggest rewarding yourself each week for the success you've had. Investing in real estate is tough, and you need to take time to enjoy it and enjoy your life.

I also suggest a slightly larger reward whenever you get a deal. Steph and I did small rewards each week, like taking Sunday afternoon off and going to see or renting a movie or spending time with friends. Every time we turned a deal into a success, we purchased some champagne and had a nice dinner.

I have a business coach right now, and one of the things he makes me do is set my goals *and* set rewards each time I hit one. The rewards get larger for the larger and more challenging goals. One of my rewards when I hit a certain goal will be to build a second home in Breckenridge. I think trips make nice rewards, too.

Take the next 30 minutes or so and write down some goals. What do you want to accomplish with your investing in the next 30 to 45 days? How about the next year and next five years? Think about the steps you need to take to get there, write them down, and place some rewards with the goals. You may want to have some large rewards, like vacations, if you reach certain goals by certain times. Maybe the reward decreases with the amount of time it takes to accomplish your goal. We talked about using mastermind groups to help hold ourselves accountable; you can also use rewards to hold yourself accountable.

Control Your Emotions

Do not let emotions sneak their creepy little heads anywhere near your business. Keep telling yourself that this is a business, and you must make your decisions based on what is best for the company.

Tenants

This is an emotional trap that is easy to get sucked into. A tenant calls with a problem and will be late with the payment. The story seems believable and probably is. The tenant asks for an additional week, then stops calling, but still has good, legitimate reasons for falling behind and a good plan to get caught up. Before you know it, there is no rent money, and it is time for the next rent payment. Maybe this month the tenant is able to pay half and asks for more time. This will go on and on.

Even though I am telling you what to watch for and how to avoid it, I can almost guarantee you will fall into this trap at least once. Let's face it, we are human, and we are sensitive to certain things like other people in need. We fell into this trap many times in the beginning, and it has cost us big-time. Please trust what I am saying here.

Stick to your guns. Sympathize with the tenant and maybe waive a late fee (although I would caution against this also), but do not stop your eviction. An eviction takes three weeks in Colorado and probably longer in other areas. This is enough time for the tenant to get you his or her rent. Start the eviction right away. Be up-front with tenants when they move in and let them know the process and how much time they have, but *do not* delay the eviction.

No pay, no stay.

Properties

Unless you are buying another home to move into, like we talked about, do not use your emotions in analyzing your deals. This has not been a problem for me, but it is for many of my clients. You may like certain areas of town, or styles of homes, colors of walls, or worse, pictures of cute kids on the wall. Please do not consider these when you are deciding if a deal can be profitable or not. Up until we separated, Steph would ask me if there were emotions involved whenever I told her I was buying another property. Makes me laugh, but it was a great way to keep me in check.

Numbers do not lie; stick to the numbers.

Sellers

This may be the toughest area for keeping emotions in check. You will find that some of the people calling you from your advertising are in desperate need and have experienced some really sad things like divorce, medical issues, loss of income, and death. We have been on appointments where the seller is crying the entire time because he or she lost a son or daughter in a car accident or were hurt at work and could no longer move around. We have had sellers begging for our help.

These appointments make you feel like you are in the right business if you can help them. The gratitude you receive is awesome. But these situations are the toughest ones for me. If you can't make a reasonable profit, don't do the deal. I know you will be in the situation and will want to help, but again, this is a business, and you must make a decision based on profit. You may bend your guidelines a little trying to help, but be very careful not to turn their problems into yours. As the saying goes, it is better to do no deals than to do a bad one.

Be Professional

Workspace
You must present yourself as a business if you ever want to build a business. If you are going to work from home, you should really have a separate part of the house dedicated to your workspace. If at all possible, have a separate room for your office.

Phone and Fax
You need to have a separate phone line that you can answer like a business and a fax line. Nothing bugs me more than a business owner who says to me, "Call before you fax anything so I can switch my fax machine over." I also lose respect for a business owner who is not home and has a voice-mail greeting from his or her kid. The easiest way to solve this is to use a cell phone that no one but you will answer and have a nice, professional greeting on your voice mail. You can also set up an online fax account like RingCentral for about $10 a month. I love this service because the faxes come to my e-mail, so I can view and print them from anywhere.

It is nice to see the faxes on my phone when they come in. Outgoing faxes are easy. You can set up a fax machine to your normal phone, or you can use a scanner with Internet fax service.

Return Calls

While we are on the subject of the phone, it is essential that you return phone calls. This sounds crazy, but as you get into business of any kind, you will find that people do not return phone calls. You will honestly separate yourself by doing this one itsy-bitsy thing. Make it a habit to return all calls the same day you get them, even if it is from a potential tenant for a house you no longer have. We have had sellers and tenants tell us that we were the only investors who called them back.

Dress

Dress appropriately for your task. Don't show up to buy someone's house dressed in flip-flops and a T-shirt. That being said, don't show up in a suit either. My suggestion is to dress business casual for everything you do, unless you are meeting with professionals who wear suits, like bankers. This is a laid-back industry, and you want to build a laid-back image. If you are too dressed up, people might view you as a shark or as the hated banker who got them into the mess. You also don't want to look like you can't afford to buy the house.

When meeting with tenants, dressing professionally is a must. It helps build credibility in the beginning, and you want to be in charge, so a suit is OK here. I don't wear suits to meet tenants, but I do dress in nice pants and a button-up shirt. It is all about perception with the tenants, so dress however you feel comfortable, as long as you are presenting a professional image.

Business Cards

Having business cards is essential. If you don't have any cards and you are meeting with sellers or going to a networking event, you can print some cards from home, but again, I suggest ordering them from a printer as soon as possible.

Business cards give people your contact information, and it is hard to throw them away. They hang around for a long time, but more than that, they build credibility. Business cards are expected to be exchanged or handed out. I use the front and back of the card. At the top of the card is "We Buy Houses." Is there any question about what I do? I also have my company name and all my contact info on the front. On the back, I list some common situations that I am looking for, and I mention that I pay referral fees to encourage referrals. Shop around to find the best deals. I have found that Vistaprint is one of the best. You can find them at vistaprint.com. If you go this direction, do not go the free business-card route. It is really tacky to have Vistaprint put their name on your card, and business cards are cheap, so just do it right.

Website

I recommend a website. It is almost unheard of for a legitimate business not to have a site. This is not essential like the business cards, so you may want to wait until you have a few deals under your belt, but don't put it off too long. Once you are more established, you can start putting some money into marketing your site. I do this for PineFinancialGroup.com and see great benefits. You can pay for leads you receive, not the number of times people see your ad, so there is a lot of value with online marketing. I am starting to get the hang of this but am by no means an expert. My suggestion is to focus on the marketing we discuss in this book, get some deals going, and then invest in your website.

Education

I can't be more serious when I say you need to invest in yourself. It is imperative to invest a percentage of all profits in you. Go to seminars, read books, listen to audio programs, and consider hiring a mentor or coach. This is something that never ends no matter how good you get or how good you think you are. I am sure you have heard it before, but there is no better return on your investment than investing in yourself. You have already shown your commitment to education by investing in this book. If you are in a market we serve, be sure to check the educational events we offer on our "Events" page at PineFinancialGroup.com.

CASE STUDIES

Case Study #1: The Tenant Nightmare

One of the most important lessons I have learned is the importance of screening tenants. I learned this the hard way with my very first tenant. Within the first year of our lease, she stopped paying. She also stopped answering her phone and returning phone calls. I had no clue what to do, so I just kept calling and writing letters. After about six weeks, I decided I needed to start an eviction.

Using a referral from other local real estate investors, I contacted an attorney and started the process. Even with the attorney and the sheriff letting her know we were going to put all her personal belongings out on the street, she decided not to move. My heart beats faster as I tell this story, because it made me so angry.

It came down to the day of the eviction, so I enrolled help from everyone I could. Steph and I took the day off from school. A few friends and my dad took the day off from work. We all went over to the property and met with the sheriff.

He walked up to the door and knocked, and my tenant came to the door with a baby in her arms. The sheriff informed her we would be removing all her stuff. She was not surprised, which surprised me. To this day, I can't understand why someone would not move out instead of having all her stuff carried to the street. And since I was upset, I was not gentle.

We went into the house and started pulling everything out. My tenant stood there and watched. This day really, really sucked. We carried out all her kids' stuff, including their toys.

I don't understand how she could not afford the rent when it looked like two full families were living in the house. It got ridiculous when we opened up the shed in the backyard and found another family living there. The shed was cozy, with an extension cord running from the house, and was fully equipped with a small bed and entertainment center. There were also about 10 car stereos that had to have been acquired illegally. Three families and a side business in stolen car stereos, and they still couldn't pay rent?

After we pulled everything out of the house, I changed the locks and left. I returned the next day to go through the house to get a feel for what needed to be done to prepare it for another tenant. When I went to the back, the back door had been pried open. According to Ricky, the gang member next door, my tenant had a bunch of stolen guns in the attic and could not get them while the sheriff was there. About half of their stuff was gone, but there was still trash everywhere. We ended up needing a roll-off dumpster to get rid of it all. There was also a car to be disposed of, and roaches were all over the place. I told Ricky he could have the car to send down to Mexico, and then I fogged my 700-square-foot house for the roaches. (Now I hire professionals to take care of roaches, because bait that only exterminators can get works so much better than foggers.)

I learned a lot of lessons from this experience. For all the properties I have and for all the years I have been doing this, I have only evicted three tenants. It's funny now that one of the three was our very first tenant, but at the time I was debating whether or not to be in this business at all.

Great Lessons from the Worst Tenant Ever

- Always screen your tenants.
- Have a clause in your lease that limits the number of people who can live there.
- Collect a large enough deposit to feel comfortable.
- Start the eviction within a week of a missed payment.
- Once the eviction is started, continue collection attempts.

Our next tenant was great. It was a Section Eight, which I have learned a lot about since then. Section Eight is a government assistance program to help low-income families pay rent. Sometimes the government will pay a portion of the rent, and often it will pay the entire amount. I was getting $1,100 in rent with a payment of $800. This is the type of cash flow we are looking for as investors. I messed this one up too, though. I thought life was great as a landlord as long as I did not hear of problems. The tenant called one time for a problem, and I did not call her back. I kept putting it off because I did not want to hear the problem, or worse, hear that she wanted to move. Because of my lack of customer service, she moved. My lesson with this tenant? Being a landlord is a customer-service business.

We cleaned it out and rented it again. This time was much better, with one exception. They lived there for over a year, they paid on time, and they took care of the place. We never received a call because whenever something broke, they fixed it. We love tenants like this. The only problem with these tenants was that they moved because they were deported back to Mexico. Before these tenants, we did not require identification, and we did not verify social security numbers. The tenants provided social security numbers, and the credit report did not indicate anything illegal. When they moved, they left a lot of trash behind. We now verify social security numbers and ask for identification. So it is OK to make mistakes. Because each time you do, you improve.

Case Study #2: Flop in Foreclosures

My friends and colleagues will tell you that I have a terrible problem referred to as the "ready, fire, aim syndrome." After going to one of those weekend-seminar sales fests, where every speaker has more to sell you than teach, we decided to invest in foreclosures. I purchased a foreclosure course that specialized in short sales. A short sale is when you buy a house from the owner of the home, but the bank allows you to pay less than the full amount owed. You are essentially creating equity by negotiating with the bank. Banks do this because it is more expensive for them to foreclose than to accept less than the full loan amount, and foreclosures look really bad on their books.

After consuming the course, Steph and I were excited to buy some houses, so we were talking to our friends and families, letting them know what we were trying to do. My brother-in-law said he had a friend who was facing foreclosure and asked that we call him. I called him up and got some basic information about the house and the situation. As soon as I got off the phone, I called my real estate coach (he came with the course) to let him know about my deal. It was tough to reach my coach because I was in school and had a job at night. We finally connected, and he suggested I get the owner to deed me the house. He suggested that we take the deed and resell the house on what we call a wrap-around mortgage. I called the seller back and let him know what I could do to help.

The way a wrap-around mortgage works is to resell a house that has an underlying mortgage without paying off the mortgage. The seller of the home—in this case, Steph and I—accepts payments from the buyer and uses the money to make the payments on the mortgage. The new mortgage, carried by the owner, wraps around the mortgage that was already in place. You can actually transfer your interest in a home and leave the loan in place. As the seller of the home, you maintain interest in the home, so if necessary, you can foreclose. This is not true if you take or give someone the deed. If you transfer title without doing a contract for deed or a wraparound mortgage, you are giving up all rights to the home even if the buyer stops making payments. For this reason, it is safe for you to buy a home by taking a deed, but it is never a good idea to sell a home this way.

Keep in mind my coach recommended this to me, but I had not even looked at the house at this point. The seller liked the idea but wanted some money for the deed. The deal was no good. He owed more than the home was worth, and his payments were too high to rent or do a wrap mortgage. For this strategy to work, you really want to collect more in a payment than you pay out each month. With that said, I also discovered that the house was in no condition to resell.

I asked the seller how much money he needed to deed us the house "as is." His response was $3,000. I had no money. Where was I going to come up with $3,000? I tried to negotiate with him, and he said another investor offered him $3,000, but he would rather sell to me since I was his friend's brother-in-law. What a load of you-know-what! No one in his right mind would have given him three grand for the deed to that worthless house, except me, of course. I fell victim to the scarcity negotiation strategy. I felt the fear of loss once he told me about his phantom investor and the phantom offer, so I felt I had to give him what he wanted if I wanted the deal. This by itself was a great lesson in negotiation.

I wanted a deal so badly that I agreed to get the money if he promised not to work with the other investor. I immediately started trying to reach my coach and started calling everyone I knew to help me get the money.

I did finally reach my coach, but I can't say I got good advice. I also found a friend, Steve, who was interested as long as I put in $1,000. So I put in $1,000, which I had to borrow, and he put in $2,000, and we took the deed to this worthless house in Denver, Colorado. For those of you familiar with the area, it was in Montbello, an area known for low-income families.

When you take a deed to a house from the owner, it is referred to as buying the property subject to the existing financing, or "subject-to." You are taking title, but you need to deal with the owner's mortgage. In most cases, you will either pay off the mortgage or make payments; otherwise, the mortgage company will foreclose and remove you from title. So even though Steve and I took title, we had a mortgage that was already in foreclosure to worry about. We were not on the loan, so the foreclosure did not go on our credit report, but it needed to be dealt with to secure our $3,000 investment.

The seller moved out, and Steve, his younger brother-in-law, Steph, and I went over to the home to start cleaning it up to resell for our huge profit. This house was trashed. Two things stick in my mind about the house.

The first was a refrigerator full of food left in the basement but not plugged in. Within seconds of opening the door, the entire house smelled like a decaying rat carcass! We needed to get that thing out of there, and it was heavy, so we tied a rope around it to keep the door closed and started to drag it up the stairs. I was on the top pulling while Steve was below pushing. Somehow the door opened, the funk flowed out, and a very small amount touched Steve. He gently let the fridge slide down the stairs until it stopped before he jumped over the fridge and ran up the stairs and outside, where he vomited all over the yard. I was close behind and almost lost my lunch when I saw that. It is funny now, but at the time we were thinking, *What the heck have we gotten into?* (Actually, watching Steve jump over the fridge in a mad dash was pretty funny then, too.)

The second thing that sticks out is that the seller left his dog locked in the garage. It was a big dog, and it was not only destroying the door trying to get out, but it would not let anyone in. Or at least nobody wanted to try to get in. Who the heck leaves their dog locked in the garage?

It did not take long—although it had already been too long—for us to realize that we were not going to be able to resell that dump and make money. I explained to Steve that we would need to talk to the bank and negotiate a short sale. According to the real estate course I studied, a short sale should have been easy to get, and we could just use hard money to finance it like the course suggested.

After about a month of talking with the mortgage company and hard-money lenders, we decided to let the mortgage company foreclose. I learned that short sales are hard work, and not every one you try will be successful. It takes a lot of short sales for one to be approved at the numbers we needed. Hard-money lenders will only lend money on homes that have a lot of equity, so it really needs to be a good deal. With our decision to let the bank foreclose, we were deciding to walk away from our $3,000 and chalk it up to an expensive lesson learned.

There were a lot of lessons from this disaster, but the biggest one was *do not* put money into a deal that you cannot get out of unless you do all your due diligence up front.

Case Study #3: Leverage Other People

Steph and I had a few lease options under our belt and were continuing to look for more property. We both worked at a bank call center. She finished work at 7:00 p.m. and would go to the gym, while I stayed at work until 9:00 p.m., when the call center closed. Steph would come back to the bank and pick me up. At least one night a week, we would leave the bank and go hang our "We Buy Homes" signs on the side of the road.

We got a phone call from a gentleman in Arvada, a suburb of Denver, and he asked us to come take a look at his house. He and his wife were recently divorced, and he wanted to move from the area. Steph and I met him at his house. He was a super nice guy, and he was happy to walk us through his house and sit down with us. The house was worth close to $200,000, he owed somewhere around $30,000, and he wanted some cash to move.

> If you are going to give the seller options, do not give them the option of saying no.

At this point in our investing, all we really knew how to do were lease options, and we did not have a clue how to talk to a seller about just buying the house. So of course, we tried to talk him into a lease option.

He liked the idea but wanted to think about it. Understand, we were not offering any money, so our solution was not really a solution for him.

I decided to call another investor I had recently met networking at a workshop to ask for a little advice. Chris was happy to hear from me and really wanted to help. I told him about our appointment and how I thought we might lose the deal. I asked for advice on what to say in the house to get the deal. Reluctantly, he agreed to go with us to the house and walk us through what to say. What a guy!

Chris showed us a strategy of making three offers all at once on a sheet of paper. The idea was to give the seller a few options to choose from, none of which included not selling the house. One offer was for cash of about $130,000, another offer was for $75,000 cash with him carrying a second mortgage of another $75,000, and the final offer was a simple lease option with us paying him $170,000 within five years.

After sitting down with him for 20 minutes, I handed him the sheet with the offers. I told him we were interested, and this is what we were willing to do.

He immediately went to the cash offer and said, "I like the idea of cash now, but this is a little low."

We instantly knew what kind of offer would work, and even though the offer was low, he did not throw us out of the house. I asked him what he was hoping for. He went on to say that he had lived in the house for 20 years with his family and knew it was worth close to $200,000. He said he was really hoping to get what it was worth. This is where I froze, and Chris finally stepped in. Chris mentioned that we are investors and need to make a profit. He also pointed out that we would need to do a little work to get the house ready to resell. Finally, Chris pointed out that he had a serious buyer in his living room right now. There was no need to list it with a Realtor and hope he could find another buyer. Chris and the seller went back and forth for a little while.

Chris finally said, "If we give you $150,000, would you take it?"

The room went silent and stayed that way for a couple of minutes. Those two minutes seemed like two weeks. It was an uncomfortable silence, but we would not budge. We made him respond.

After a few minutes of agony, for everyone, the seller said "Yes."

Chris reached over and shook his hand and said, "Congratulations, you just sold your house." A big smile appeared on the seller's face. This experience really helped me realize that as investors, we are providing a valuable service. Chris sent me to the car to get an agreement, and we put the house under contract.

Afterward, Steph, Chris, and I went to a restaurant close by to have a drink and talk about our success. Chris asked us how it felt to make $10,000 to $15,000 within the last hour. He explained that you always make your money in real estate when you buy, and we'd just purchased a house at a great bargain.

Steph and I spent the next few weeks cleaning up the place and painting. We then started marketing for a buyer. It took about three months, but we finally found a buyer and moved him in. We let him rent until he closed on the new loan. He was not a well-qualified buyer, but Chris knew a great mortgage broker, and together they got him qualified, and the deal closed.

Chris mailed us half of the profit in the amount of $16,869!

There were a lot of lessons with this deal, too. This was the first real success we'd had and the first time we saw any true profit. The only tool we'd had in our belt was the lease-option strategy. When your only tool is a hammer, all you see are nails. As you progress with your investing, you will notice you need a variety of tools so that when a deal presents itself, you will know how to structure it. You must start somewhere, and you can't expect to learn everything on your own or all at once. We started with lease options because they are easy to get into, and it gave us the confidence to find this seller. We did not know the best way to structure the deal, so we asked for help. Chris walked us through the deal and gave us a template for how to do it on our own next time. We found the deal and brought it to Chris, and he made almost $17,000. Was that a good deal for him? Was it a good deal for us? It was a great deal for him and for us because he made money with about an hour of his time invested, and we learned lessons to help us succeed. It is hard to put a price on learning tools that will make you rich.

Here is a copy of the check Steph and I got from the case study above.

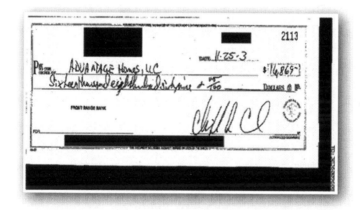

APPENDIX

It is recommended that you seek legal advice before using any of these documents.

Lease Option FRBO Phone Script

(Phone rings.)

SELLER: Hello?

YOU: Hello, my name is _____. I am calling about the home you have for rent. Is it still available?

SELLER: Yes, it is.

YOU: Can you tell me a little about the home? (bedrooms, baths, etc.) (*If he or she asks what you would like to know, say, "I don't know. How many bedrooms and baths does it have? What is your favorite feature? How do you like the area?"*)

SELLER tells you about some of the features.

YOU: Wow! Sounds like a great home. How long of a lease are you looking for?

SELLER tells you the length of the lease.

YOU: Great! I am actually looking for a long-term lease of at least two years. Is that OK?

Seller answers.

You: Assuming all payments are on time, would you ever consider selling the property at the end of the two years?

Seller: *(If he or she says no, hang up; if he or she says yes, keep going.)*

You: Great! Now, I am an investor looking to buy homes in decent neighborhoods *(or say whatever you want)*. Can you tell me, is your home in a decent neighborhood?

Seller answers.

You: I would really like to set up a time to see the home. What is a good time for us to get together?

Seller answers.

You: That sounds good. Now, are you the owner of the home?

Seller answers.

You: I will see you *(repeat the day and time)*. Just one last question…sounds like such a great home, why would you ever even consider selling?

Seller answers.

You: OK, I look forward to meeting you.

Lease Option FSBO Phone Script

(Phone rings.)

SELLER: Hello?

YOU: Hello, my name is_____. I am calling about the home you have for sale.

SELLER: Yes?

YOU: Yes. Is it still available?

SELLER: Yes, it is.

YOU: Great! Can you tell me a little about the home? (bedrooms, baths, etc.) *(If he or she asks what you would like to know, say, "I don't know. How many bedrooms and baths does it have? What is your favorite feature? How do you like the area?")*

SELLER tells you about some of the features.

YOU: Wow! Sounds like a great home. Why would you ever even consider selling it?

SELLER: I lost my job and am downgrading.

YOU: I am so sorry to hear that.

SELLER: It is OK, but thank you.

YOU: I would really like to set up a time to see the home. What is a good time for us to get together?

SELLER gives you a time.

YOU: That sounds good. Now, are you the owner of the home?

SELLER answers.

YOU: I will see you *(repeat the day and time)*. I look forward to
        meeting you.

Seller Phone Script

(When you are returning their call from your marketing)
(Phone rings.)

SELLER: Hello?

YOU: Hello, may I speak with _____?

SELLER: This is her/him.

YOU: Hello, my name is _____. I am returning your call about the home you have for sale.

SELLER: Yes?

YOU: Do you have a couple of minutes?

SELLER: Sure.

YOU: I am just curious—how did you get my number?

SELLER: I noticed a sign on the side of the road.

YOU: Great! Can you tell me a little about the home (bedrooms, baths, etc.)? *(If he or she asks what you would like to know, say, "I don't know. How many bedrooms and baths does it have? What is your favorite feature? How do you like the area?")*

SELLER tells you about some of the features.

You: Wow! Sounds like a great home. Why would you ever even consider selling it?

Seller tells you the reason. *(Get as much information as you can to complete your Seller Call Sheet. Ask the seller if he or she has another home, when he or she is moving, if the seller is living there now, what he or she is trying to sell it for, what it is worth, what he or she owes, and payments, etc. If it is a rental, ask what it rents for and about the tenants, etc.)*

You: It sounds like a great home that I would be interested in taking a look at. Are you the only decision maker, or is there someone else on title with you?

Seller: My husband/wife is also on title.

You: When is a good time for the three of us to get together and view the home?

Seller answers.

You: I will see you *(repeat day and time).* I am looking forward to meeting you.

Seller Call Sheet

How did you hear about us? Date:_____/_____/_____
Flyer
Mailings Sign
Internet
Referred by _____
Other _____

Personal

Name: _____

Phone: _____ Alt. Phone: _____

Mailing Address: _____

Property

Property Address: _____

Vacant: Y/N How Long: _____ Year Built: _____

Rental: Y/N Rent Amount: _____ Beds/Baths/Garage: _____

Sq. Ft.: _____ Extras: _____

Motivation

Why Selling: _____

Where Moving: _____ When: _____

Plans if property does not sell: _____

Additional Information: _____

Asking Price: _____ Value: _____ Appraisal Realtor Guess

1st Mortgage: _____ Payment: _____ P I T I ARM: Y/N

2nd Mortgage: _____ Payment: _____ P I T I ARM: Y/N

Lease Option Agreement

This agreement, dated _____, is between _____, the Landlord, and _____, the Tenant.

In consideration of the payment of rent and the keeping and performance of the covenants and agreements by Tenant hereinafter set forth, Landlord does hereby lease unto Tenant, the following described premises situated in the County of _____, State of _____, to wit:

With a street address of:

_____

The said premises, as described above, are hereby leased to Tenant for a term of _____ months commencing _____. Rent for the premises is payable in monthly installments of $_____, to be paid by the _____ day of the month for which rent is due. $_____ of each on time rent payment shall be credited toward the purchase price of the property. Payments to commence _____. This Agreement shall automatically renew for _____ additional 12-month periods following the expiration of the initial term unless Tenant gives thirty (30) days' notice prior to any renewal.

Tenant agrees as follows:

1. To pay the rent for said premises as hereinabove provided.
2. To keep said premises in good condition and repair and at the expiration of this lease to surrender and deliver up the same in as good order and condition as when entered upon, loss by fire, inevitable accident, act of God, or ordinary wear and tear excepted.

It is further mutually agreed that if Tenant shall be in arrears in the payments of any installment of rent, or any portion thereof, or in default of any covenants and agreements herein contained to be performed by Tenant, which default shall be uncorrected for a period of Ten (10) days after Landlord has given written notice thereof, Landlord may, at his option, without liability for trespass or damages, in any manner as allowed by law, declare the term of this lease ended; repossess the said premises as of Landlord's former estate; and peaceably expel and remove Tenant, those claiming under him, or any person or persons occupying the same and their effects, all without prejudice to any other remedies available to Landlord for arrears of rent or breach of covenant.

It is further mutually agreed that Landlord, in consideration of the performance of all the covenants and agreements herein to be performed by Tenant under the lease, and for Tenant agreeing to perform all minor repairs to the property during the term of the said lease, hereby grants to Tenant an exclusive option to purchase the above described premises at any time during the term of this lease or any renewals for the sum of $_____payable as follows:

as full payment for Landlord's equity. The Landlord, upon payment of said purchase money, shall convey said premises by, and warrants that only those liens listed herein exist and that no additional liens will be placed against the property during the term of this agreement. Current balance due of any encumbrances are as follows:

_____

Landlord shall also furnish a policy of title from a reputable title insurance company at his expense so showing.

Provisions:

1. **Utilities:** Tenant agrees to pay all water, sewer, gas, and electric charges incurred during his/her tenancy.

2. **Maintenance:** Tenant shall be responsible for all maintenance and repairs as needed or requested by Tenant that do not cumulatively exceed $_____ per month. Any amount of the above repairs over $_____ per month shall be paid by Landlord. If Landlord cannot or will not make the repairs as specified in this agreement within ten (10) days of notice, then Tenant will have the option of either voiding this agreement by written notice to Landlord or making such repairs and receiving a credit toward any future payments due Landlord.

3. **Title:** Landlord shall execute a Deed of Trust or Mortgage and Option Affidavit in favor of Tenant to secure performance of this agreement. At closing, costs shall be split equally between the parties.

4. **Inspection:** This agreement is subject to a final inspection and approval of the property in writing by Tenant prior to taking possession.

5. **Assignment:** The original Tenant shall be permitted the right of subletting or assignment without Landlord's written permission. Any successive tenant wishing to assign this agreement must have written permission of Landlord. If this agreement is assigned, Tenant shall be released from any further liability hereunder, and the Assignee(s) will accept all responsibilities, privileges, covenants, conditions, and obligations as set forth in this entire Agreement.

6. **Access:** Tenant shall have immediate access with a key to show the property to contractors, prospective tenants, and other interested parties. In the event property is not vacant on the commencement date listed above, then at Tenant's option all dates in this agreement may be moved into the future one month (delay period) for each and every month the property is not vacated by current occupant. After 99 delay periods, this agreement shall expire.

7. **Illegal Provisions:** Whatever item in this Agreement is found to be contrary to any local, state, or federal law shall be considered null and void, just as if it had never appeared in this Agreement, and it shall not affect the validity of any other item in this Agreement.

8. **Insurance:** Landlord shall pay for and maintain fire and extended-coverage insurance on said property for full replacement value of the property, naming Tenant as an additional insured. In the event the property is destroyed in whole or in part, Landlord shall repair the property as fast as possible at his expense, and an equitable part of the rent shall be abated until so repaired.

9. **Qualified Resident:** This agreement is subject to Tenant approving a qualified resident to occupy the property.

_____   _____
Landlord   Date   Tenant   Date

STATE OF _____)

COUNTY OF _____)S.S.

On _____ before me,

personally appeared _____ ,

personally known to me (or proved to me on the basis of satisfactory evidence) to be the person(s) whose name(s) is/are subscribed to the within instrument and acknowledged to me that he/she/they executed the same in his/her/their authorized capacity (or capacities) and that by his/her/their signature(s) on the instrument the person(s), or the entity upon behalf of which the person(s) acted, executed the instrument.

WITNESS my hand and official seal.

Signature _____

MY COMMISSION EXPIRES:

Lease Option Agreement (Completed Sample)

This agreement, dated ___**November 1, 2015**___, is between ___**Sally Seller**___, the Landlord, and ___**Advantage Homes, LLC**___, the Tenant.

In consideration of the payment of rent and the keeping and performance of the covenants and agreements by Tenant hereinafter set forth, Landlord does hereby lease unto Tenant, the following described premises situated in the County of ___**Somewhere**___, State of ___**Anystate**___, to wit:

LOT 21, BLOCK 4, OF SOMEWHERE REALLY FUN, COUNTY OF SOMEWHERE, STATE OF ANYSTATE

With a street address of:
1234 Main St Somewhere, Anystate, 98765

The said premises, as described above, are hereby leased to Tenant for a term of ___**12**___ months commencing ___**November 1, 2015**___. Rent for the premises is payable in monthly installments of $___**1,000.00**___, to be paid by the ___**1st**___ day of the month for which rent is due. $___**100.00**___ of each on time rent payment shall be credited toward the purchase price of the property. Payments to commence ___**December 1, 2015**___. This Agreement shall automatically renew for ___**9**___ additional 12-month periods following the expiration of the initial term unless Tenant gives thirty (30) days' notice prior to any renewal.

Tenant agrees as follows:

1. To pay the rent for said premises as hereinabove provided.
2. To keep said premises in good condition and repair and at the expiration of this lease to surrender and deliver up the same in as good order and condition as when entered upon, loss by fire, inevitable accident, act of God, or ordinary wear and tear excepted.

It is further mutually agreed that if the tenant shall be in arrears in the payments of any installment of rent, or any portion thereof, or in default of any covenants and agreements herein contained to be performed by Tenant, which default shall be uncorrected for a period of Ten (10) days after Landlord has given written notice thereof, Landlord may, at his option, without liability for trespass or damages, in any manner as allowed by law, declare the term of this lease ended; repossess the said premises as of Landlord's former estate; and peaceably expel and remove Tenant, those claiming under him, or any person or persons occupying the same and their effects, all without prejudice to any other remedies available to Landlord for arrears of rent or breach of covenant.

It is further mutually agreed that Landlord, in consideration of the performance of all the covenants and agreements herein to be performed by Tenant under the lease, and for Tenant agreeing to perform all minor repairs to the property during the term of the said lease, hereby grants to Tenant an exclusive option to purchase the above described premises at any time during the term of this lease or any renewals for the sum of $ __*200,000.00*__ payable as follows:

Cash at closing

as full payment for Landlord's equity. The Landlord, upon payment of said purchase money, shall convey said premises by, and warrants that only those liens listed herein exist and that no additional liens will be placed against the property during the term of this agreement. Current balance due of any encumbrances are as follows:

Wells Fargo for approximately $147,000.00

and Landlord shall furnish a policy of title from a reputable title insurance company at his expense so showing.

Provisions:

1. **Utilities:** Tenant agrees to pay all water, sewer, gas, and electric charges incurred during his tenancy.
2. **Maintenance:** Tenant shall be responsible for all maintenance and repairs as needed or requested by Tenant that do not cumulatively exceed $___*200.00*___ per month. Any amount of the above repairs over $___*200.00*___ per month shall be paid by Landlord. If Landlord cannot or will not make the repairs as specified in this agreement within ten (10) days of notice, then Tenant will have the option of either voiding this agreement by written notice to Landlord or making such repairs and receiving a credit toward any future payments due Landlord.
3. **Title:** Landlord shall execute a Deed of Trust or Mortgage and Option Affidavit in favor of Tenant to secure performance of this agreement. At closing, costs shall be split equally between the parties.
4. **Inspection:** This agreement is subject to a final inspection and approval of the property in writing by Tenant prior to taking possession.
5. **Assignment:** The original Tenant shall be permitted the right of subletting or assignment without Landlord's written permission. Any successive tenant wishing to assign this agreement must have written permission of Landlord. If this agreement is assigned, Tenant shall be released from any further liability hereunder, and the Assignee(s) will accept all responsibilities, privileges, covenants, conditions, and obligations as set forth in this entire Agreement.
6. **Access:** Tenant shall have immediate access with a key to show the property to contractors, prospective tenants, and other interested parties. In the event property is not vacant on the commencement date listed above, then at Tenant's option all dates in this agreement may be moved into the future one month (delay period) for

each and every month the property is not vacated by current occupant. After 99 delay periods, this agreement shall expire.

7. **Illegal Provisions:** Whatever item in this Agreement is found to be contrary to any local, state, or federal law shall be considered null and void, just as if it had never appeared in this Agreement, and it shall not affect the validity of any other item in this Agreement.

8. **Insurance:** Landlord shall pay for and maintain fire and extended-coverage insurance on said property for full replacement value of the property, naming Tenant as an additional insured. In the event the property is destroyed in whole or in part, Landlord shall repair the property as fast as possible at his expense, and an equitable part of the rent shall be abated until so repaired.

9. **Qualified Resident:** This agreement is subject to Tenant approving a qualified resident to occupy the property.

Kevin Amolsch, Member 11/1/15   **Sally Seller 11/1/15**

_____   _____
Landlord   Date   Tenant   Date

STATE OF **_Anystate_** _____)

COUNTY OF **_Anywhere_** _____) S.S.

On **_11/1/2015_** _____before me,

personally appeared **_Sally Seller_** _____,

personally known to me (or proved to me on the basis of satisfactory evidence) to be the person(s) whose name(s) is/are subscribed to the within instrument and acknowledged to me that he/she/they executed the same in his/her/their authorized capacity (or capacities) and that by his/her/their signature(s) on the instrument, the person(s), or the entity upon behalf of which the person(s) acted, executed the instrument.

WITNESS my hand and official seal.

Signature **Some Great Notary**

MY COMMISSION EXPIRES**: 5/15/2021**

Addendum A to Lease Purchase Agreement

Between _____, the Landlord,

and _____, the Tenant.

Dated _____

_____

_____

_____

_____

_____

_____

_____

_____

_____

_____

| Landlord | Date | | Tenant | Date |

RECORDING REQUESTED BY:

WHEN RECORDED, AND UNLESS OTHERWISE
SHOWN BELOW, MAIL TAX STATEMENTS TO:

SPACE ABOVE THIS LINE FOR RECORDER'S USE

Option Affidavit

Be the world hereby apprised that I/we_____(Optionor)
have granted to_____(Optionee)
an exclusive option to purchase the following legally described property:

Anyone dealing in and with the subject property should contact Optionee
at:

Regarding the terms of option to purchase and the parties' respective
rights thereunder.
IN WITNESS WHEREOF, the parties have signed this agreement.

STATE OF   )   _____
COUNTY OF   ) S.S.   Optionor
On_____before me,
_____,

personally appeared _____,

personally known to me (or proved to me on the basis of satisfactory evidence) to be the person(s) whose name(s) is/are subscribed to the within
instrument and acknowledged to me that he/she/they executed the same

in his/her/their authorized capacity (or capacities) and that by his/her/their signature(s) on the instrument, the person(s), or the entity upon behalf of which the person(s) acted, executed the instrument.

WITNESS my hand and official seal.

Signature ————————————————————————

MAIL TAX STATEMENTS AS DIRECTED ABOVE.

MY COMMISSION EXPIRES:

Additional Insured Letter

To Whom It May Concern:

I (we) hereby notify and request that_____(Insurance

Company) list_____as an "additionally insured" on

my (our) home owner's insurance policy for the property located at:

_____

(Policy number: _____)

I (we) have come to a financial arrangement with_____regarding

this property and have agreed to maintain the adequate homeowner's insurance to cover all parties' interests should there be a loss.

Any changes to this request must be signed both by me (us) and_____

_____. I (we) also give you permission to openly discuss any aspect of my

(our) insurance regarding this property with_____from this day forward.

Furthermore, I (we) authorize to upgrade my (our) existing policy or make other changes that he/she feels necessary to protect his/her financial interest in the property.

You may accept either a copy or a fax of this authorization as an original.

Sincerely,

_____   _____   _____

Home Owner (print)   Sign   Date

Social Security # _____ - _____ - _____

_____   _____   _____

Home Owner (print)   Sign   Date

Social Security # _____ - _____ - _____

Address of Additionally Insured:

_____

_____

_____

Purchase and Sale Agreement

_____, as Seller,
and _____ or assigns as Buyer,
hereby agree that the Seller shall sell and the Buyer shall buy the following described property UPON THE TERMS AND CONDITIONS HEREINAFTER SET FORTH, which shall include the STANDARDS FOR REAL ESTATE TRANSACTIONS set forth within this agreement.

1. LEGAL DESCRIPTION
   Commonly known as_____
2. PURCHASE PRICE _____Dollars.
   (a) Deposit to be held in trust by _____ $ _____
   (b) Approximate principal balance of first mortgage to which conveyance shall be made
       subject to, if any, Mortgage holder:_____ $ _____
   (c) Other: _____ $ _____
   (d) Other: _____ $ _____
   (e) Cash or certified or cashier's check on closing and delivery of deed (or such greater or lesser amount as may be necessary to complete payment of purchase price after credits, adjustments and prorations). $_____
3. PRORATIONS: Taxes, insurance, interest, rents, and other expenses and revenue of said property shall be prorated as of date of closing.
4. ACCESS: Buyer shall be entitled a key and be entitled to access property to show partners, lenders, inspectors/contractors, and other interested parties prior to closing. Buyer may place a sign on the property prior to closing to help Buyer find end user for property.
5. EXECUTION IN COUNTERPARTS: This agreement may be executed in counterparts and by facsimile signatures. This agreement becomes effective as of the date of the last signature.

6. DEFAULT BY BUYER: If the buyer fails to perform any of the covenants of this contract, all money paid to Seller by Buyer as aforesaid shall be retained by or for the account of the Seller as consideration for the execution of this contract and as agreed liquidated damages and in full settlement of any and all claims for damages.

7. DEFAULT BY SELLER: If the Seller fails to perform any of the covenants of this contract, the aforesaid money paid by the Buyer, at the option of the Buyer, shall be returned to the Buyer on demand; or the Buyer shall have the right of specific performance.

8. CONVEYANCE: Seller to deliver to Buyer Fee Simple title by a General Warranty Deed free from any liens, restrictions, encumbrances, or easements not specifically referenced in this agreement. Seller expressly agrees and understands that buyer is taking title subject to the existing financing described above, and is not expressly assuming responsibility for the underlying loans. If the actual loan balance of above loan(s) is less than stated herein, the purchase price shall be reduced to reflect this difference. If the actual loan balance(s) is more than stated herein, then Buyer's required cash payment shall be reduced accordingly. Seller agrees to waive tax and insurance escrows held by said lender(s) or his/her/their assigns.

9. INSPECTIONS: Buyer or his agent may inspect all appliances, air conditioning and heating systems, electrical systems, plumbing, machinery, sprinklers, and pool system included in the sale. Seller shall pay for repairs necessary to place such items in working order at the time of closing. Within 48 hours before closing, Buyer shall be entitled, upon reasonable notice to Seller, to inspect the premises to determine that said items are in working order. Unless specifically excluded in this agreement, all other items of personal property located in or on the property shall be included in the sale or shall be transferred by Bill of Sale with warranty of title. Seller expressly warrants that property, improvements, buildings

or structures, the appliances, roof, plumbing, and heating and/ or ventilation/air conditioning systems are in good and working order. This clause shall survive closing of title.

10. LEASES: If this is an income property, Seller shall provide Buyer with an accounting and assignment of security deposits at closing. Seller agrees to defend and indemnify Buyer for any and all claims, judgments, and lawsuits related to the wrongful withholding of security deposits that arose out of events or circumstances arising before closing of title. This clause shall survive closing of title.

11. NO JUDGMENTS: Seller warrants that there are no judgments threatening the equity of this property, and that there is no bankruptcy pending or contemplated by any title holder. Seller will not further encumber the property and an affidavit may be recorded at Buyer's expense putting the public on notice that the closing of this contract will extinguish liens and encumbrances hereafter recorded.

12. CLOSING: Closing shall be held on or about _____, 20_____, unless extended no more than 60 days by either party in writing, at a time and place designated by Buyer. Buyer shall choose the escrow, title, and/or closing agent.

13. TIME IS OF THE ESSENCE: Time is of the essence of this agreement. Parties will diligently pursue the completion of this transaction.

14. DOCUMENTS FOR CLOSING: Buyer shall pay for preparation of deed, note, mortgage, any corrective instruments required for perfecting the title, and closing statement and shall submit copies of same to Seller at closing.

15. EXPENSES: State documentary stamps required on the instrument of conveyance, the cost of recording any corrective instruments to title, and title insurance shall be paid by the Seller. Documentary stamps to be affixed to the note secured by the purchase money mortgage, intangible tax on the mortgage, and the cost of

recording the deed and purchasing money mortgage shall be paid by the Buyer. All other closing costs shall be split 50/50.

16. INSURANCE: As consideration for this purchase the Seller will assign all insurance policies on this property to the Buyer and will grant to Buyer a limited power of attorney to deal with the lender(s) and insurance provider(s) with respect to this property.

17. RISK OF LOSS: If this property is damaged prior to transfer of title, Buyer has the option of choosing to either accept any insurance proceeds with the title to the property in "as is" condition, or canceling this agreement and accepting the return of all deposits.

18. MAINTENANCE: Between the date of contract and the date of closing, the property, including the lawn, shrubbery, and pool, if any, shall be maintained by the Seller in the condition as it existed as of the date of the contract, ordinary wear and tear to be expected.

19. DEFECTS: Seller warrants subject property to be free from hazardous substances and from violation of any zoning, environmental, building, health, or other governmental codes or ordinances. Seller further warrants that there are no material or other known defects or facts regarding this property that would adversely affect the value of the property. This clause shall survive closing of title.

20. TYPEWRITTEN OR HANDWRITTEN PROVISIONS: Typewritten or handwritten provisions inserted in this form shall control all printed provisions in conflict therewith.

21. OTHER AGREEMENTS: No agreements or representations, unless incorporated in this contract, shall be binding upon any of the parties.

22. SPECIAL CLAUSES:

_____   _____

Seller   Date   Buyer   Date

_____   _____

Seller   Date   Buyer   Date

Authorization to Release Information

Authorization dated _____

Borrower(s): _____

Lender name: _____

Loan No.: _____

Property: _____

I/We the undersigned hereby authorize you to release information regarding the above referenced loan to _____
its agents and/or assigns. This form may be duplicated in blank and/or sent via facsimile transmission. This authorization is a continuation authorization for said persons to receive information about my loan, including duplicates of any notices sent to me regarding my loan.

_____   _____   _____

Borrower   Date of Birth   Social Security Number

_____   _____   _____

Borrower   Date of Birth   Social Security Number

Direct-Payments Authorization

If the mortgage payments, property taxes, association fees, insurance pre-miums, or other property
payments on_____
ever go into arrears, then_____(Landlord) hereby
gives_____(Tenant) or his/her/its assigns or heirs the right to make
payments directly to the lender or other party who is owed payment on
Landlord's behalf.

Any payment sent on Landlord's behalf will be considered rent (or other
money due) in compliance with Residential Lease Purchase Agreement
between these parties dated_____.

To adequately compensate the Tenant for the additional risk incurred by
making such payments of additional rents and costs, for every one dollar
($1) paid to lender or other parties to make up late payment(s) and/or fee,
premiums, etc., three dollars ($3) shall be credited off the option price
stated in the Lease Purchase Agreement.

Once these payments/fees are made current, Tenant may make his or her
payments directly to the Lender and other parties for the remainder of the
lease period stated in the Residential Lease Purchase Agreement. These
continuing payments sent directly to the lender or other parties shall be
considered as rent (or other money due) received by Landlord in compli-ance with Residential Lease Purchase Agreement but shall not be credited
with the three-for-one credit detailed above.

Payments will be mailed to the following lender(s):

_____

Lender One

_____

Lender Two

_____

(Lender's Address)

_____

(Lender's Address)

_____

(Lender's City, State, Zip)

_____

(Lender's City, State, Zip)

_____

(Lender's Phone Number)

_____

(Lender's Phone Number)

_____

Landlord

_____

Date

_____

Landlord

_____

Date

Resident Call Sheet

1st Contact Date   Property Calling About

Name_____Area Interested In_____

Phone_____Beds/Baths_____

Alt. Phone_____Current Rent_____

Address_____Afford Monthly_____

City/State/Zip_____Up-Front Payment/Deposit_____

Occupation_____How Many Will Live There_____

Spouse Occupation_____When Moving_____

Credit Rating (1–10)_____Follow-Up_____

Monthly Income_____

How did you hear about this property? _____

1st Showing Date_____Time_____

NOTES:

_____

_____

_____

_____

_____

_____

_____

_____

Rent-to-Own Price Sheet

Property Address: _____   *Length of Lease: 2 Years*

Option 1		Option 2		Option 3	
Rent:	$1,695	Rent:	$1,695	Rent:	$1,695
Rent Credit:	$50	Rent Credit:	$200	Rent Credit:	$500
Total Rent Credit:	$1,200	Total Rent Credit:	$4,800	Total Rent Credit:	$12,000
Starting Price:	$299,950	Starting Price:	$299,950	Starting Price:	$299,950
Option Payment:	$7,000	Option Payment:	$7,000	Option Payment:	$7,000
Total Credits:	$8,200	Total Credits:	$11,800	Total Credits:	$19,000
Final Price:	**$284,750**	**Final Price:**	**$281,150**	**Final Price:**	**$273,950**

Six Reasons Rent to Own Works For You:

1. **Rent Credits:** Each month a big chunk of your rent goes toward the purchase of your home, allowing you to build equity in your home faster than a traditional mortgage—no more wasting money on rent.

2. **Improving Your Property:** Because you will own this property soon, any improvements you do that increase the value of the property help you build more equity for yourself.

3. **No Banks to Deal with**—no more bank hassles!

4. **Own Your Own Home:** You enjoy the benefits of owning your home *before* you technically ever buy it!

5. **Flexibility:** You have total flexibility: you have the *option* to buy your home, not the obligation!

6. **Your Credit:** You are creating a strong credit reference while you are renting to own!

Note: *All current and future values of property are projected estimates and may or may not come to pass. No one can accurately predict the future value of any given property, and you understand the risks related to this fact.*

Rental Application

Property Address:_____

To guarantee compliance with the Federal Fair Housing Acts, a separate $20.00 non-refundable processing fee is required for each person adding income to this application.

Current monthly rent or house payment_____Date you would like to move_____

Length of desired occupancy_____Number of people who will occupy the property_____

The money I have available **today** to apply toward moving into this property is $_____.

Name_____Soc. Sec. #_____-_____-_____

Home phone_____Work phone_____Cell Phone_____

Driver's Lic. #_____E-mail address_____

Name (co-app)_____Soc. Sec. #_____-_____-_____

Home phone_____Work phone_____Cell Phone_____

Driver's Lic. #_____E-mail address_____

Residence History

Address_____City_____State_____Zip_____

How long at present address?_____Occupancy dates_____Why moving_____

Landlord's Name_____Phone #_____

Former Address_____City_____State_____Zip_____

How long at present address?_____Occupancy dates_____Why moved _____

Landlord's Name_____Phone #_____

Employment History (Last 2 Years)

Current Employer   Start Date

Address_____City_____State_____Zip_____

Position\Job description_____Monthly gross income_____

Supervisor's Name and position_____Phone #_____

Current Employer (co-app)_____Start Date:_____

Address_____City_____State_____Zip_____

Position\Job description_____Monthly gross income_____

Supervisor's Name and position (co-app)_____Phone #_____

Former Employer_____Start Date:_____

Address_____City_____State_____Zip_____

Position\Job description_____Monthly gross income_____

Supervisor's Name and position_____Phone #_____

Former Employer (co-app)_____Start Date:_____

Address_____City_____State_____Zip_____

Position\Job description_____Monthly gross income_____

Supervisor's name and position_____Phone #_____

Emergency Contact: Failure to pay rent is an Emergency!!

_____ _____ _____ _____

Name   Address   Phone   Relationship

LIST ALL PETS THAT YOU DESIRE TO LIVE ON THE PREMISES

Pet's name: Type\Size   Sex\Neutered\Spayed   Indoor\Outdoor

1. _____

2. _____

REFERENCES

Name   Address   Phone   Relationship

1. _____

2. _____

3. _____

CIRCLE ALL THAT APPLY

Personal Skills: 0 Plumbing 0 Carpentry 0 Painting 0 Electrical 0 Mechanical 0 Other **Tools you Own:** 0 Tool Box 0 Mower 0 Yard Tools 0 Snow Shovel 0 Vacuum Cleaner

Are you interested in owning a home?   0 Yes 0 No

If we can qualify you for a home loan with payments you can afford, would   0 Yes 0 No

you like to buy now?

When would you like to buy? 0 Now 0 6 months 0 1 year 0 2 years 0 more than 2 years

Have you ever been evicted from any tenancy?   0 Yes 0 No

Have you ever willfully and intentionally refused to pay rent when due?   0 Yes 0 No

Do you have anything that may interrupt income or ability to pay rent?   0 Yes 0 No

Have you ever filed a petition of bankruptcy?   0 Yes 0 No

Are you required to pay child support or alimony?   0 Yes 0 No

If yes, how much?_____

Applicant hereby certifies that all information in this application is true and correct to his or her best knowledge. Applicants also hereby authorize Landlord to verify this application through an Investigative Report and a Credit Report. **A non-refundable fee of $20.00 for processing is required for each person adding income before verification can begin.** Applicants understand that they will not receive a copy of the credit report.

Applicants authorize present and past Landlords, Employers, Banks, References, and any other persons to release information regarding applicant's credit, rental, and employment histories. A copy of this Authorization may be accepted as an original.

_____	_____	_____
Date	Applicant's Signature	Date of Birth

_____	_____	_____
Date	Applicant's Signature	Date of Birth

Deposit Receipt

This form is to serve as a receipt for a deposit received by
_____ in the amount of $ _____.
This deposit is to hold Prospective Tenant's position to rent to own or buy
the property located at: _____

_____

All of Prospective Tenant's deposit will apply toward the purchase of said
property and is considered part of the Option Payment.

This deposit is non-refundable, and Prospective Tenant must pay an additional $_____ option consideration by _____

and the first month's rent of $_____ before moving
into the property on _____. If either of these payments are
not received by Landlord on time, then Landlord may cancel the agreement, and all money paid to Landlord by Prospective Tenant shall be kept
as liquidated damages. These payments must be certified funds.

This agreement is subject to Landlord's final approval of Prospective
Tenant's application. In the event that Landlord does not approve Tenant
for any reason, Landlord will refund all of Prospective Tenant's deposit and
cancel this agreement.

Prospective Tenant understands that Prospective Tenant does NOT have a
valid lease or option to purchase said property UNTIL Prospective Tenant is
approved and makes both other payments described above on time and signs
all further paperwork with Landlord, including Lease Agreement, Option to
Purchase Agreement, Disclosure Forms, etc. In no case may the Prospective

Tenant enter or otherwise occupy said property until ALL conditions and terms in this agreement have been fulfilled. TIME IS OF THE ESSENCE!

_____   _____

Prospective Tenant   Date

_____   _____

Landlord or Agent for Landlord   Date

Rental Agreement

1. On_____,_____
   (Tenant), agrees to rent the dwelling located at:_____
   (_____ County) from_____(Landlord). The term of
   this shall begin on _____and end at noon on
   _____.

2. Landlord is the agent for service of notice on this property and
   may be contacted by mail at:

   _____

   _____

   _____

   Office address is subject to change by written notice. All cor-
   respondence between the parties of this agreement shall be in
   writing.

3. RENT: The amount of the rent will be $_____ . Tenant un-
   derstands and agrees that if the total rent is not received by the
   _____of each month at 5:00 p.m., there will be a **6%** late
   charge in addition to the full rent due. If rent is received after the
   _____of the month or late fees and/or "additional rents" as
   defined herein are not included with such payment, rent will be
   considered "unpaid." Any payments received by Landlord will be
   applied first toward late fees and/or other additional charges, then
   toward rent. The acceptance by Landlord of partial payments of
   rent due shall NOT, under any circumstances, constitute a waiver
   by Landlord, nor affect any notice or legal proceeding. If a check is
   returned by Tenant's bank for any reason, Tenant understands and
   agrees that there will be a **$40.00** returned-check charge in addi-
   tion to the full rent and late charges due. In addition, Tenant will
   have to pay using cashier's checks or money orders from then on.
   Your rent payment is critical! No excuses will be accepted
   for nonpayment including ill health, accident, loss of job, financial problems, family emergencies, etc.! **FAILURE TO PAY RENT**

WHEN DUE WILL RESULT IN IMMEDIATE TERMINATION OF THIS RENTAL AGREEMENT AND EVICTION. There will be a standard **4%** rent increase beginning on _____.

4. USE: The property will be used only as living quarters for the following people:

_____   _____

_____   _____

$100.00 additional rent will be due each month for any other persons occupying the premises for a period longer than seven (7) days, and written permission must be obtained in advance for additional Tenants. Otherwise Tenant will be in default and will be charged $100.00 per month for each additional occupant retroactive to the day he or she began tenancy. Tenant agrees that premises will not be used for day care or babysitting.

5. DELIVERY OF RENTS: Landlord accepts rent in the following ways:
   - Delivery by mail.
   - Landlord will pick up rent ($25 Charge).
   - Check by phone ($10 charge).
   - Auto draft from Tenant's checking account.

   Checks sent by mail are done so at the sender's own risk. Rents will be credited as paid only when actually received by Landlord. If you would prefer to mail your rent, it is recommended it be mailed at least one week early to allow for any delay in delivery and sent to the address at the beginning of this agreement. If you would prefer, the Landlord will pick up rent for a $25 fee. Landlord also accepts payments by phone with a valid checking account for a $10 fee, or you can pay rent by auto payment. Please ask Landlord for information on auto pay. Remember, if rent is lost in the mail, it has not been paid!

6. UTILITIES: Tenant is responsible for payment of all utilities including, but not limited to: electricity, garbage, water, sewer, gas, telephone, and cable TV charges incurred during tenancy and thereafter until he or she terminates these services. Tenant

specifically authorizes the Landlord\Agent to charge Tenant for all unpaid amounts as *additional rent*. Tenant shall not allow electricity or other utilities to be disconnected or discontinued for any reason and by any means (including nonpayment of bill) until the end of the lease term or renewal period.

7. Tenant will notify Landlord\Agent within three (3) days of any changes of phone number.

8. RECEIPT OF MONIES BY LANDLORD: Tenant and Landlord hereby agree that all monies received by Landlord or its agents shall first be applied to any and all charges due other than rent, and then and only then the balance of any monies received shall be applied toward rent due. Remember, if your rent is lost in the mail, it has not been paid.

9. SECURITY DEPOSIT: There is a $ _____security deposit that has been paid as a condition of or as a part of this lease. This security deposit may NOT be applied by Tenant to the final month's rent or any other sum due under this agreement without the written permission of the Landlord. Within 30 days after Tenant has vacated property and left it in "broom clean" condition, removed all personal possessions and rubbish, returned all keys, and provided Landlord with forwarding address, Landlord will give to Tenant an itemized written statement of the reasons for any deductions to, and the amounts of, the Tenant's security deposit, along with a check for any balance due.

10. ACCEPTANCE OF PROPERTY: The property is accepted in its current state of cleanliness and will be returned in the same approximate condition. If you wish to pay a $150.00 extra cleaning fee to have hired maids clean the property prior to moving in, the Landlord\Agent will arrange it. The Tenant has been given the opportunity to fully inspect the property and warrants that the property being rented is hereby accepted as being in good and safe condition together with all furnishings unless a written exception is delivered to the Landlord\Agent within three (3) days after signing

this agreement. Only those items included in said written exception shall be accepted as defective, missing, or in need of remedial action. The absence of such notice shall be conclusive proof that there was no defective or hazardous equipment or conditions existing as of the start of the tenancy. An inspection and inventory record may be written up by Tenant for the purpose of documenting any defects as well as the serial numbers and description of appliances and personal property located on the premises. This will establish the baseline condition of the property and the property inventory for which the tenant will be held accountable. Only after this record has been filled in and delivered to Landlord within the above three-day time limit will necessary action be initiated to make any needed repairs. Any defects noted after the first three days will be presumed to have been caused by Tenant. TIME IS OF THE ESSENCE IN RETURNING THIS INFORMATION.

11. PETS: Landlord agrees to allow all pets listed on the rental application.

12. MOTOR VEHICLES: Tenant and Landlord agree that any abandoned, unlicensed, derelict, and/or inoperable vehicles parked on the premises may be towed off the premises by Landlord at the vehicle owner's expense after posting a 72-hour notice in a conspicuous place on the vehicle indicating Landlord's intent to tow said vehicle. Tenant further agrees not to store and/or park any trailer, camper, boat, or any other similar recreational item or vehicle on the premises without the written consent of Landlord. Tenant agrees not to store and/or park any commercial or public vehicle on the premises under any conditions. Tenant further agrees not to make any repairs on motor vehicles of any type while such motor vehicles are on or within 200 feet of the property.

13. RULES AND REGULATIONS: Tenant, Tenant's guests and occupants shall comply with written unit rules (including community policies), which shall be considered part of this lease. Landlord may make reasonable rule changes if put into writing and delivered to

Tenant. Changes are effective immediately. Tenant shall be liable to Landlord for damages caused by Tenant or Tenant's guests or occupants. Sidewalks, steps, entrance halls, walkways and stairs shall not be obstructed or used for any purpose other than ingress or egress.

14. DISORDERLY CONDUCT: Tenant agrees not to permit or suffer any disorderly conduct, noise, vibration, odors or other nuisance whatever about the Property, having a tendency to annoy or disturb any persons occupying adjacent Properties and to use no machinery.

15. MAINTENANCE: Tenant shall take an active role to insure that the property stays in excellent condition. Landlord is not responsible for damage caused by the Tenant. Tenant agrees that he/she has had adequate opportunity to inspect the conditions of the property and Landlord makes no warranties or representations about the condition of the property, the improvements, utilities, electrical, plumbing, appliances, any latent defect of property, or the neighborhood. Tenant will NOT make any major alterations to the property without prior written consent of Landlord. Tenant is required to obtain any and all necessary permits required by law before commencing improvement. Any work performed on the premises whether by Tenant or other parties shall be as an independent contractor or agent of Tenant and not an employee or agent of Landlord. Tenant further warrants that he/she will be accountable for any mishaps and/or accidents resulting from such work, and will defend, indemnify, and hold harmless Landlord and Landlord's agents free from claims of any other person or entity. All improvements to the property shall be the property of the Landlord and remain attached and a part of the property when the Tenant vacates. If there are any needed repairs in excess of $200 in one month, Landlord agrees to pay the amount over the first $200. Tenant is responsible for the first $200. Tenant will have any

maintenance requests submitted in writing and any request must be approved by Landlord in writing.

SMOKE DETECTORS: As part of this tenancy, Tenant shall supply and maintain smoke detector(s), carbon monoxide detector(s), and fire extinguisher(s). Tenant agrees to test smoke detector(s) and carbon monoxide detector(s) on a regular basis and to change batteries as necessary. Tenant agrees that any blockages in plumbing and drains or any broken glass that is not revealed on the inspection and inventory record at time of move in are the full responsibility of Tenant regardless of cause. Tenant agrees to make a diligent effort to repair any hazardous conditions as quickly as possible.

16. PAYMENT OF FUTURE RENT: In the event of the failure of Tenant to pay any rents or other monetary obligations due hereunder, Landlord, besides other rights and remedies he may have, at his option, may either terminate this lease, or from time to time without terminating this lease, relet the Property. Upon such re-letting, all rentals and other sums received by Landlord from such re-letting, shall be applied first to the payment of debt other than rent due to Landlord; second, to costs and expenses of re-letting; third, to past due rent, with the residue, if any, to be held by Landlord and applied as payment of future rent as the same become due and payable hereunder. No such re-entry or retaking possession of said Property by Landlord shall be construed as an election on his part to terminate this lease unless written notice of such intention be given to the Tenant or unless the termination hereof be decreed by a Court of competent jurisdiction.

17. ABANDONMENT: Formal written notice, with provision for timely rent payment, is required if there will be an intended absence. If the premises appear to be unoccupied for 15 days while rent is due and unpaid, and Tenant has not given Landlord\Agent written notice as to his/her intentions, then the Landlord\Agent is authorized

to take immediate possession. He will place the Tenant's property into storage at a site of the Landlord's choosing at the Tenant's expense not to exceed $20 per day. Property left unclaimed more than 15 days shall be presumed to have been abandoned. The Tenant herein gives the Landlord\Agent specific authority, without recourse, to dispose of the abandoned property in any manner the Landlord\Agent chooses that does not violate applicable statutes, without any recourse whatsoever on the part of Tenant, as full liquidated damages for lost rents or damages sustained by the Landlord\Agent because of said abandonment.

18. ASSIGNMENT: Tenant shall not assign this Agreement or sublet the Property or any part thereof and shall not allow any person to occupy the same, other than persons to whom the Property is rented under this Agreement, without prior written consent of Landlord.

19. ACCESS: Tenant shall allow Landlord access at all reasonable times to the Property for the purpose of inspection, to make repairs that have been requested by the Tenant, or to show the Property to prospective purchasers, mortgagees of the Property, or to any other person having a legitimate interest therein, or to make necessary repairs or improvements. Landlord shall not, unless requested in writing, give Tenant notice prior to entering the Property for routine situations requiring access to the Property. Tenant agrees that in case of emergency or apparent abandonment, Landlord may enter the Property without consent of Tenant.

20. RE-RENTING ACCESS AND FEE: In the event this agreement is terminated prior to the date stated in paragraph 1, or should a 30-day written notice to vacate not be submitted as required herein, the parties to this agreement agree that the Landlord/Agent shall be deemed to be damaged in re-rental costs difficult to determine. To cover expenses including but not exclusive of those for advertising, bookkeeping, and leasing fees, it is agreed that a re-rental fee equal to the then-current monthly rental amount less

$5.00 will be assessed to Tenant as liquidated damages for the aforementioned expenses. Tenant agrees that Landlord shall have the right to show the Property to prospective tenants at reasonable times for a period of thirty (30) days prior to expiration of this tenancy or upon having received written notice from Tenant of an intention to vacate. Landlord shall, whenever practical, give Tenant 24 hours' notice.

21. LEGAL COSTS: If the Tenant desires to continue to rent the premises after being in default or after being served for eviction or with notice of termination, he/she agrees to reimburse the Landlord/Agent for actual costs incurred to enforce collection of rents, serve notices, for filing fees, etc., including costs of collectors, deputies, marshals, police constables, etc., prior to regaining entry or reinstatement of Tenant status. In the event of any legal dispute involving the courts, in consideration of the mutual covenants expressed herein, both Tenant and Landlord/Agent warrant that each will pay his/her own legal costs and expenses of lawyers and court costs etc., and hereby hold the other harmless for such costs.

22. NOTICE TO QUIT AND HOLDOVER: TENANT AGREES, AT LEAST THIRTY (30) DAYS PRIOR TO THE EXPIRATION OF THE DATE IN PARAGRAPH 1, TO GIVE WRITTEN NOTICE TO AGENT OF THE INTENTION TO VACATE THE SUBJECT PROPERTY AT THE END OF THE TERM OF THE LEASE. AND IF SUCH NOTICE IS NOT TIMELY GIVEN, THE TENANT SHALL BE LIABLE FOR AND AGREES TO PAY TO THE AGENT, THE RENT DUE FOR THE FOLLOWING MONTH IF THE SUBJECT PROPERTY IS NOT RE-RENTED. In the event that the Tenant holds over the Property after the term of the Rental Agreement, the same shall be deemed to be month-to-month residency, with an increase of 20% in the monthly rental amount due, with all other provisions of the Rental Agreement, including the provision requiring at least thirty (30) days' notice of Tenant's intention to vacate upon the expiration of the lease term, shall remain in effect. Tenant agrees that unless a

notice to vacate is received on the first of a given month, the effective date of such notice shall be the first of the following month.

23. LIABILITY: Landlord and Tenant further agree that Owner or Landlord will not be liable for any damages or losses to person or property caused by other Tenants, or persons, theft, burglary, vandalism, or other crimes. Landlord or Owner shall not be liable for personal injury or for damage to or loss of Tenant's personal property (furniture, jewelry, clothing, etc.) from fire, flood, water leaks, rain, hail, ice, snow, smoke, explosions, interruption of utilities, or acts of God unless same is due to negligence of Owner or Landlord. Landlord strongly recommends that Tenant secure his/her own insurance to protect against all of the above events. Tenant has inspected existing locks and latches and agrees they are safe and acceptable. Landlord shall have no duty to furnish alarms of any kind, security guards, or additional locks and latches. Tenant shall NOT make any changes or additions to the existing locks for any reason without Landlord's written permission.

24. POSSESSION: If Landlord\Agent is unable to deliver possession of the premises within seven days of the commencement date stated above, then this contract may be terminated at Landlord's option and all funds received from Tenant will be returned. Tenant agrees to hold Landlord\Agent harmless for any further obligations and/or consequential damages.

25. In the event any portion of this contract shall be found to be insupportable under the state statutes in which the property is located, the remaining provisions shall continue to be valid and subject to enforcement in the courts without exception. In like manner, any obligations of either Landlord\Agent or Tenant that may become law shall be binding on both parties as if included herein. All rights granted to Landlord\Agent by Tenant shall be cumulative and in addition to any new law, which might come into being. Any exercise, or failure to exercise, by the Landlord\Agent of any right shall

not act as a waiver of any other rights. **This contract represents the total agreement between the parties hereto.** No other terms or conditions shall have any effect unless endorsed herein in writing and initialed by the parties.

26. JOINT AND SEVERAL LIABILITY: It is understood and agreed that each party signing this Rental Agreement is liable for the full amount of any and all financial obligations herein and is further agreed that each and all of the signors herein are jointly and severally liable for any and all financial obligations.

27. **By signing this rental contract you stipulate and warrant that all questions have been answered and that you thoroughly understand all provisions as to the rights, duties, and obligations of all parties.** Further, you swear to pay the rent on time, maintain the property, and fulfill all your obligations hereunder or face the full financial and legal consequences of default and termination. You expressly warrant that you have the legal right to bind all occupants and to sign for them in committing yourself and them to this rental contract. NOTE: TIME IS OF THE ESSENCE IN ALL PROVISIONS OF THIS RENTAL CONTRACT.

28. ADDITIONAL PROVISIONS:

_____

_____

_____

_____

_____   _____

Landlord or Agent for Landlord   Date

_____   _____

Tenant   Date

_____   _____

Tenant   Date

Option Agreement

On this_____day of_____,_____Landlord agrees that_____

_____(Tenant(s)) has the option to purchase the property located at:

for the price of $_____under the following terms and conditions:

1. The non-refundable option payment of $_____will apply in full to the purchase price at closing. In the event Tenant fails to exercise this option or defaults under any terms of the attached Rental Agreement, then this option will be void and all monies paid to Landlord by Tenant will be retained by Landlord as liquidated damages and not as a penalty.

2. The term of this agreement is_____months running concurrently with the attached Rental Agreement, and all of the terms and conditions of the Rental Agreement must have been complied with in order for this option to be valid. Tenant understands that if he/she does not comply with ALL terms of Rental Agreement, then this option agreement is not valid. This includes (but is not limited to) paying the rent on time each month and taking care of all the maintenance as described in the Rental Agreement. If Tenant ever substantially defaults on the payments or terms of said Rental Agreement, this option to purchase will automatically void and any monies paid to Landlord for rent or option consideration will be retained by Landlord as liquidated damages and not as a penalty. **NOTE: A substantial default includes, but is not limited to, failure to make any rent payment due on said lease within 15 days of the due date for that rental payment.**

3. Each month that the rent is paid on time, starting on_____ and ending with rent paid through_____, Tenant shall receive a non refundable credit of $_____ to reduce the

option price of the property if Tenant exercises Tenant's option to purchase.

4. Rent is considered to have been paid on time if and only if it is **received** by Landlord by 5:00 p.m. of the_____day of the month for which it is due. Any acceptance of a late rent payment from Tenant to Landlord shall NOT qualify as an on time rent payment nor shall it be a waiver of any rights of the Landlord on this or any other agreement between Landlord and Tenant.

5. There will be no real estate commission paid as a result of this transaction, and Tenant will be responsible for all closing costs other than documentary stamps on the deed. This option is subject to Landlord's ability to transfer clear title to the property. Taxes and insurance will be prorated as of the date of this agreement. Landlord will credit tenant $100.00 at closing toward title insurance.

6. The recording of this option or any memorandum thereof will result in the automatic revocation of this option, and all monies paid to Landlord by Tenant shall be retained by Landlord as liquidated damages and not as a penalty. In addition, Tenant will be liable to Landlord for all incidental and consequential damages for slander of title, including, but not limited to, attorney fees and court costs for correcting title.

7. Any changes Tenant wishes to make to the property prior to closing must be approved by Landlord in writing. Any improvements made by Tenant will become a part of the property and may not be removed by Tenant in the event of any default on the part of Tenant. In no case shall the Tenant be entitled to any consideration for making any improvement or addition to the property for any reason.

8. This property is being transferred in "as is" condition. Tenant acknowledges that he/she has inspected the property and accepts it in current condition. Tenant is responsible for all repairs and maintenance during this agreement.

9. Tenant acknowledges that Landlord has made no representations or warranties concerning the condition of the property or the improvements thereon, its ownership, the neighborhood, or the value of the property. Landlord may hold legal title to property, have equitable title via a land contract, or may have a lease with option to purchase property. In the event Landlord cannot perform on this option for any reason, Landlord shall return to Tenant all option consideration paid as detailed in paragraph 1 as full and complete liquidated damages.

10. To exercise this option, Tenant must give Seller written notice at least 90 days before this option expires. In the event that Tenant does not give written notice of Tenant's intention to exercise this option to purchase said property, and this written notice is not received by Landlord at least 90 days prior to the option's expiration date, then this option is null and void. This option expires on _____. This option is NOT contingent upon Tenant's ability to obtain financing from a lender or for any other reason. Tenant understands that TIME IS OF THE ESSENCE for this agreement and that Tenant's failure to purchase the property before the expiration of this option, for any reason, or Tenant's default on any of the terms or conditions of the attached Rental Agreement shall make this option void. In this case, all option monies received by Landlord shall be kept by Landlord as liquidated damages. This agreement is NOT an installment sale or land contract or contract-for-deed agreement; it is merely an option-to-purchase agreement about the above-referenced property under the terms and conditions stated in this agreement. Said notice shall be mailed or delivered to: _____

11. All parties to this agreement have read and fully understand its provisions and hereby acknowledge the receipt of a signed copy of this agreement. Tenant is encouraged to seek the counsel of an attorney if he/she does not fully understand any part of this agreement. Furthermore, Tenant acknowledges that he/she

understands that Landlord relied on Tenant to get Tenant's own legal advice from a qualified source.

12. Additional Provisions:

Landlord or Agent for Landlord	Date
Tenant	Date
Tenant	Date

Receipt for Inventory Checklist and Lease

Tenant acknowledges receipt of two inventory checklist forms and a signed copy of the lease for the premises located at _____. If one completed checklist is not returned to Landlord within seven (7) days after obtaining possession of the rental unit, Landlord and Tenant may assume that no real or personal property on the premises is damaged or flawed in any respect.

_____   _____

Landlord or Agent for Landlord   Date

_____   _____

Tenant   Date

_____   _____

Tenant   Date

Landlord/Resident Checklist

GENERAL CONDITION OF RENTAL UNIT AND PREMISES

Address_____

LIVING ROOM	Condition on Arrival	Condition on Departure
Floors & Floor Coverings		
Walls & Ceilings		
Windows, Screens & Doors		
Light Fixtures		
Front Door & Locks		
Smoke Detector		
Fireplace		
Drapes & Window Coverings		
Other		
KITCHEN		
Floors & Floor Coverings		
Light Fixtures		
Walls & Ceilings		
Cabinets		
Counters		
Stove/Oven		
Refrigerator		
Dishwasher		
Garbage Disposal		
Sink & Plumbing		
Smoke Detector		
Other		
DINING ROOM		
Floors & Floor Covering		
Walls & Ceilings		
Light Fixtures		
Windows, Screens & Doors		
Smoke Detector		
Other		

Kevin Amolsch

BATHROOM (S)	Condition on Arrival			Condition on Departure		
	Bath 1	Bath 2	Bath 3	Bath 1	Bath 2	Bath 3
Floors & Floor Coverings						
Walls & Ceilings						
Windows, Screens & Doors						
Light Fixtures						
Bathtub/Shower						
Sink & Counters						
Toilet						
Other						
Other						
BEDROOM (S)	Bdrm 1	Bdrm 2	Bdrm 3	Bdrm 1	Bdrm 2	Bdrm 3
Floors & Floor Coverings						
Windows, Screens & Doors						
Walls & Ceilings						
Light Fixtures						
Smoke Detector						
Other						
Other						
Other						
OTHER AREAS						
Heating System						
Air Conditioning						
Lawn/Garden						
Stairs & Hallway						
Patio, Terrace, Deck, etc.						
Basement						
Parking Area						
Other						
Other						
Other						

190

Made in the USA
San Bernardino, CA
24 March 2016